AMERICAN LABOR

FROM CONSPIRACY
TO
COLLECTIVE BARGAINING

LIFE OF RICHARD F. TREVELLICK, THE LABOR ORATOR

[Obediah Hicks]

ARNO & THE NEW YORK TIMES
NEW YORK   1971

Reprint Edition 1971 by Arno Press Inc.

Reprinted from a copy in
The State Historical Society of Wisconsin Library
LC# 77-156418
ISBN 0-405-02926-8

American Labor: From Conspiracy to Collective Bargaining—Series II
ISBN for complete set: 0-405-02910-1
See last pages of this volume for titles.

Manufactured in the United States of America

LIFE OF

Richard F. Trevellick,

THE LABOR ORATOR

RICHARD F. TREVELLICK.

LIFE OF

Richard F. Trevellick,

THE LABOR ORATOR,

OR THE

Harbinger of the Eight-Hour

System.

———

1896.

J. E. WILLIAMS & CO., PRINTERS AND BINDERS.

JOLIET, ILLINOIS.

TABLE OF CONTENTS.

PREFACE.

IN writing up the life and work of Captain Trevellick, of Detroit, the writer wishes to show to the working men of America and Brittain how much of good may be accomplished by systematic and persistent effort, when purely unselfish methods are adopted. I shall try to state the plain facts as I have gathered them from my personal observation or from the information which I have obtained from Mr. Trevellick himself. Also quote from his own writings on Labor and Finance and rely on the testimony of others to show the capabilities of the man. Possibly some of the dates used may not be strictly correct.

...WITH EULOGIES BY...

 JOHN McLAUCHLIN,
 SEYMOUR F. NORTON,
 FRANCES E. WILLARD,
 ROBT. SCHILLING,
 M. DANDO,
 SAMUEL GOMPCRO,
 EUGENE V. DEBS,
 GEO. A. SCHILLING,
 JOHN RYAN,
 RALPH BEAUMONT,
 SAMUEL LEAVITT.

CHAPTER I.

RICHARD F. TREVELLICK was born on St. Mary's Isle, one of the group of the Scilly Islands, which lie about thirty miles southwest of the Land's End, County of Cornwall, England. These islands lie at the entrance of the English and Irish, or St. George's Channels. The coast being very rocky and extremely dangerous, many disastrous shipwrecks have occurred on these rocks and numerous lives have been lost. In 1707 Sir Cloudsley Shovell's squadron of war ships struck these rocks, and three ships were wrecked and all the crews—several hundred men—were drowned. Only a few years ago the Atlantic liner, Schiller, went to pieces at the same place and three hundred persons were drowned.

The Islands were called the Casseritides in ancient times and were visited by the ships of Tharshish when they came to Cornwall for tin, copper and other valuables for King Solomon

Some valuable stone for building, resembling marble, was taken from the Islands, of which only a few chippings now remain. The Celtic or Phonecian crews of those ships and their friends settled in those Islands and on the Cornish and Welsh coasts and from them Trevellick descended on his father's side.

All the names of persons and places beginning with Tre, Pen and Pol, of which there are very many, such as Tregarthan, Trevellian, Trezise, Tremaine, Penrose, Penberthy, Pengally, Polglaize, Polperro, Polraun, and hundreds of others, were derived from the Cymric branch of the Celtic race which seemed to originate in Phonecia, north of Palestine.

The house in which he was born stands in a flower and fruit garden at the foot of Rocky Hill, in a beautiful little vale, with the thatched roof almost covered by climbing roses and other flowering vines. The fragrance of the gilliflowers, wallflowers, roses and other flora, cultivated by the mother and sister and the fruit bloom of the orchard cherished by the father, at the rear of the house, made it a delightful abode in the spring and summer time. The whole islands are now one vast flower bed from which London gets hundreds of tons of cut flowers every summer. The house being only a short distance from the sea shore, the wild scream of the sea mew on the rocks was Trevellick's lullaby, and the sweet song of the sky lark, as it rose from the meadow with joy to meet the rising sun coming up over the ocean, awoke him from his slumbers, and as he sallied forth to milk the cow in the meadow the cuckoo sounded its charming notes amid the hawthorn bloom on a May morning.

Trevellick's father was a meek and kind old man who loved to talk of American freedom, he having resided some time at Silver Lake in New York about 1812. The only thing he did not like in the United States were the periodical money panics. In one of them he lost all of his wages which he had left in the care of his employer to accumulate. Soon after he buried two brothers there, and then went back on the old farm in St. Mary's, on which his ancestors had lived and died for over 700 years or about the time of King John 1166-1216. Trevellick had three brothers and one sister. All of them are now dead but one brother, William, who is one of the leading floriculturists of those Islands. Trevellick's mother, a descendant of the old English aristocracy, was well formed, dignified in manner, with much firmness and decision of character.

As will be seen in this narrative, Trevellick, or for short we will call him Dick, as that was what his comrades called him both in England and in this country, inherited a great deal of his mother's disposition of independence and firm resolve. About his fourteenth year he went apprentice to be a joiner, but in about three years his master died. For a short time he worked on the farm and the writer once saw him wielding the scythe, cradling grain for the neighboring farmers, but he soon went into Mr. Mumford's shipyard to learn that trade, and soon became an expert workman. At twenty-one, in the year 1851, he went to Southampton and helped to build a large ship for the South American trade, called the Parana. A memorable year was 1851, the first world's exhibition in London, the winning of the Queen's cup by the yacht America at the Isle of Wight, and the one in which Dick started the Eight Hour agitation.

It was done in this way. Dick belonged to a

debating or mutual improvement society at Southampton. It was composed of some of the best class of clerks and business men, some civil and marine engineers and a few carpenters and others. I was then living in that city and one evening he told me that he proposed the following question for debate: "Resolved; that the workingmen of Brittain would be benefitted by adopting an eight hour work day." The debate took place and was a lively contest, Dick there showing that he was a natural orator. The local paper published the debate in full and it being a new idea and such arguments as Dick produced in its favor, one of the London dailies reprinted it and at the next session of Parliament some member introduced a resolution in favor of eight hours, but of course in that body it was voted down at once.

But the ball was started rolling and still continues to roll, Gladstone and other high officials of England and Herbert Bismark of Germany favoring it. Many trades unions of England are adopting the system. In America all employes of the general government are working under that system and several states have eight hour laws on their statute books, while many thousands of workmen in the trades unions are adopting the system.

CHAPTER II.

DICK was always a strong temperance advocate, and so were his father and brothers.
While in Southampton Dick joined a vegetarian
society, and he ate no meat or fish for nearly a
year. He was strong and healthy, and at that time
might be termed a handsome young man, full of
life and repartee; he dressed in the latest fashion
and was a good, moral, church-going man, a good
entertainer and could play some music, so he had
no trouble to get into good society.

One evening he came to visit the writer at
our boarding house, where four of us carpenters
boarded. Our landlady was a widow with two
children. Her husband had been a chief engineer
of a steamship and had left her in pretty good
circumstances, but she was a worker and a smart,
vivacious woman, and when Dick was introduced
to the lady he was invited to take tea the following Sunday, which invitation of course our gal-

lant accepted.   Well, the time came and we were well entertained by the lady in the parlor in the evening with singing and music.   Before leaving Dick had accepted an invitation to accompany the lady to her church, St Mary's Episcopal, the following Sunday morning.   He called in on the Saturday evening following, ostensibly to play a game of seven-up with us boarders, but more to show us a new frilled bosomed shirt, new necktie and some pocket handkerchiefs and black kid gloves, which, he gave us to understand, were purchased for his room mate as he was not as good at selecting such things as he was.   The landlady was not present when he called as she was entertaining some visitors up in the parlor, so the hired girls told us, and Dick went home with his parcel.   Soon after he left there came a knock at the basement door, and a dressmaker called in to see Mrs. Spargo, with a new black silk dress to try on, but as Mrs. Spargo, the landlady, could not be seen that night, the woman said she would bring the dress early Sunday morning, and went away.   Soon we wished to retire and the girl gave us a light.   On ascending the stairs we met a man coming down with our bed in his arms.   Of

course we stopped him until he explained that the
furniture was his and he and his man were taking
it for an amount that had not been paid on the
goods.   We rushed down stairs to find that the
policeman had taken our landlady to jail an hour
previous.

The men took all but the parlor and kitchen
furniture and left at 11 o'clock at night.   There
was a dilemma; no beds for us or the hired girls!
So we all sat by the fire the balance of the night.
Early next morning we moved our trunks next
door, the girls took the children to their uncle's
and the house was locked up.   But soon came the
fun.   About nine o'clock—a fine summer morning
—up ran our young hero dressed in swallow tail
coat, white vest, light pants, plug hat, frilled
shirt, gold shirt studs, kid gloves and walking
stick, and politely knocked at the front door.   As
we were laying for him, we soon had the joke on
him.   He was dumbfounded.   "Great God, what
a lesson in the frailties of human nature."   But
worse than all, his brother was one of our number and certainly would not keep the secret.

The woman was tried and convicted and sen-
tenced to the penitentiary for one year for obtain-

ing 40 yards of silk at the silk mercer's under
false preteuses. She had pawned half of the silk
and had bought plated ware to be used at dinner
on returning from church. The other silk was
in the dress, which I think the dressmaker re-
tained. She had bought the silk on credit to
make mourning dresses for herself and mother,
whose brother, General Smith, had died in the
Isle of Wight, she said. The goods were sent to
her address. As the mercer had not heard of the
death of the General by the papers, he stepped
in next door to ask the upholsterer if he had heard
of the general's death, and told of sending the
silk to a certain number in Latimer street. Aha,
that was where he had furnished those beds and
furniture nearly six months before and could get
no money. They started an agent to make in-
quiries in the Isle of Wight. 'Twas all a hoax.
No such general had died there and the warrant
was sworn out with the above results. Poor
woman! she had risked her reputation to catch
Dick; she played her trump card and lost. Alas
for human nature.

The next week Dick's brother Sam and the
writer went to Portsmouth to work for Mr.

Thomas White on his dry dock. One Sunday
Dick came over to pay us a visit, and see the great
naval and military rendevouz of Great Brittan.
After attending church, and dining with us,
we spent a pleasant afternoon, and at eight
o'clock we went with him to the depot. He
entered the compartment car and took a seat in
the corner. Just then a young man entered and
took a seat. He was followed by a large old
gentleman with a very red face, who was in a
towering passion. The young man was his
nephew and enquired the cause of his uncle's
wrath. He stated that an infernal pauper had
been begging from. him and that his pension as a
retired naval commander could not support him in
his station in life and maintain paupers. Trevellick then asked him what a pauper was. He
turned a withering glance at Dick and told him
he must be very ignorant not to know that. He
said that a pauper was an imposter on the public
and did not work and got a shilling per day from
the Relief Funds. Dick made a mental calcula-
tion and said: "I find that you do not work and
get a hundred pounds or more per year; therefore
you are more of an imposter than twenty paupers.'

Up went that great walking stick, and it would have reached Dick's head only it struck the roof of the car. Then a wordy war ensued till they reached Southampton. On leaving the car the old man said, "Well, I see you know more than I thought you did, and I would like to debate more with you and show you your folly." Dick said, "I will meet you in any public hall in the city, but I don't want to meet you in a dark alley, for you might murder me with that stick." "What! By the memory of Lord Nelson. Me a murderer!" Dick had to clear out quick and left the old man foaming with rage and his nephew trying to quiet him.

Dick soon finished his job on the Parana and returned to Scilly for a visit, quite a dashing young man. The girls were on the qui vive. Dick took a liking to one, Mary, and seemed to love her company very much. Having had a good time with all his friends and relatives, he was about to leave home again to make his fortune and come home to marry the girl of his choice, when his mother got up a farewell party but did not invite Mary, as she did not deem her worthy and dignified enough for her favorite son's company. Dick insisted that Mary must come to the party or he would not be there himself. But Greek had met Greek and there was no surrender on either side. His mother claimed to be mistress in her own house, and would not surrender. So the party was had, and Dick had business elsewhere. He told his mother to prepare his clothes for he should leave home in the morning and she would never see his face again. (And she never did.)

Morning came, good byes were spoken and Dick started for London to get a berth as carpenter of a ship, a position for which he was well adapted. He soon found one and sailed for Calcutta. The second mate becoming sick, Dick took his place, and one night in the tropics as they were running down along the African coast with the trade winds and fine weather, all sails set, a circumstance took place that Dick could account for only in telepathy. He had gone into his stateroom, lighted his hanging lamp and lay on his bed to read a short time, as at eight bells —eight o'clock—he would have to take charge of the watch on deck. As he lay deeply engrossed in his book, he suddenly became impressed by

some indefinable presence. He turned his eyes to
the door and saw a woman's form going out the
half opened door. He started up, but the apparition vanished. It was Mary's form, color of hair,
and the dress she wore when he last saw her.
He turned down the leaf of the book and went
into the cabin, looked at the chronometer and log
book, came back and entered the day and time
with the latitude and longitude on the page where
he was reading, and donning his heavy coat and
southwester hat, he lighted his cigar and went
on deck and took charge, while he kept up a great
deal of thinking.

They soon had rough weather in rounding
Cape of Good Hope and his mind was engaged in
taking care of the ship; and in going up the
Indian Ocean Dick studied the navigator's art of
finding his way over the trackless ocean. In a
few weeks they arrived in Calcutta all right.
Awaiting him were letters from home, arrived by
steamer. Yes, and one from Mary. Oh, what
joyful news that letter contained! On the same
day and on the same hour (as near as he could
figure it out in the difference of time in that latitude) that he saw the apparition, Mary received

a message from his mother to visit her at her
home. She went, and the old lady embraced her
and cried over her and told her she was welcome
any time and in the future she would treat her as
a daughter.

Of course Dick was overjoyed, but he must
make that fortune to make Mary a rich woman,
so he soon left there in the same ship for Melbourne, Australia, and got there in 1852, just in
all the gold excitement. Thousands of emigrants
were rushing there from all quarters, and scores
of ships were being deserted by their crews. As
a ship carpenter he got work in the shipyard.
One day he met a woman he had known in Scilly,
his home, and on inquiring why she was there,
she told a sad tale of suffering and want. Husband sick in bed, all money gone and she was in
despair. He inquired who she was married to.
She answered, John Fairchild, who had been
Dick's old shop mate in the joiner's shop at home.
He went to the house forthwith, and spoke words
of cheer to them, and before he left he placed
twenty sovereigns in the woman's hand. She
hesitated to take it, but he insisted that he could

soon earn more—and he did. The man soon got well and went earning money himself.

Dick went to New Zealand, where at Auckland he helped to organize the Eight-hour League. They took it into politics, and the system became a law of that colony. Dick's eloquence helped the agitation wonderfully. The prime movers were the shipwrights and caulkers. After that he took a chief mate's berth on a ship for India and China, and while lying in the harbor of Akyab waiting for a cargo, the crew of the ship was stricken with cholera (as were many other ships' crews). The doctors ordered brandy in large doses, but Dick would not allow the men to take intoxicating liquor as he believed it would do more harm than good, and he had his own way as the captain was sick on shore himself. The result was that he did not lose a man, while the other ships lost most of their crews.

In 1854 he was back in Melbourne, organizing the eight hour movements, aud in 1857 it became the law of those colonies.

CHAPTER III.

DICK spent most of 1853 in the gold regions with varied success. At one time he, in company with forty other prospectors, wandered so far away in the mountains of Australia that they got lost for several days. Provisions and water ran short. If they found water containing fish or frogs they drank it, but other water often contained mineral that was injurious. For food they killed parrots and sometimes a kangaroo. A parrot was excellent eating for a hungry man. They found some gold, but not in paying quantities, and they returned to town ragged and unkempt and unshorn. They camped a few miles outside and cast lots which two of them should go in town for decent clothes for the rest. Dick and a son of a British naval officer were chosen to go, and next morning they marched up the steps of one of the large hotels and wanted to stop there to dinner. The servant turned the dirty tramps

away with the expression that they had no time
to spare with them as they were going to have a
select party to dinner that day.

They then went to a gents' furnishing store
and asked the proprietor to get them entire out-
fits of fashionable clothes, boots, hats and canes.
They went into a back room and in came a neighboring barber and went to work on them, and in
two hours two young gents went up those same
hotel steps dressed in high style. The landlady
met them at the door and ushered them in with
the greatest politeness. She was so glad of their
company—as they had a select party to dinner
and a ball at night. Dinner was soon ready and
our young gents sat one on each side of the landlady at the head of the table. They told the
guests that they had late· news from the gold
mines, as they had recently been there, when of
course they were the lions of the evening. After
dinner was most over Dick asked the lady if they
had seen two dirty looking tramps at her door in
the forenoon. She said there was, but that she
despised such creatures and took it as an insult
for them to come to her house, and especially to
the front door. Dick asked her if she would

recognize those two men again. Of course she
would if she saw them. "Well," says Dick, "we
are the men." She waited to hear no more, and
she did not attend the ball, either. They paid
their bill to the clerk next morning and were soon
on their way back to camp with the outfit for the
other men. MORAL:—Don't take a man by his
looks, nor a parson by his books.

At another time while with another company
digging with shovel and rocker, a little uniformed
fellow walked up and placed Dick under arrest
for digging without a license. Dick told him to
produce his warrant and he shoved a loaded revolver under his nose. Dick being some distance
from camp was not armed, so he had to go ahead
of that revolver. In going through a lonely piece
of woods where several murders and robberies
had been committed, Dick thought "who knows
but this fellow is in disguise and has brought me
here to murder and rob me of the gold in my
belt." He watched a chance and snatched the
revolver from him, then turned him round and
walked him back to camp. A council of men
was held and they ordered him out of camp and
to protect himself they returned him his revolver

and gave him only a few minutes to get out of
sight. He went. But in a day or two an officer
came with a warrant for the whole party. They
were marched up before the Colonial or government judge and charges preferred of digging
without a license and resisting an officer.

The judge said the offenses were very grave,
in the demoralization of the people at that time of
great excitement, but he wished to hear the excuse of the prisoners. Dick asked the privilege
of pleading the case, as they had no lawyer there
to act for them. He was permitted to do so, and
then told his story and launched out in oratory on
the liberty of the British subject as allowed in
the Magna Charta. At the close of the plea the
judge ordered the discharge of the prisoners and
strongly reprimanded the officer for not showing
his warrant when demanded. He said he felt
proud of any British subject that had the courage
to defend his life and liberty as Dick had done.
"Call the next case."

They had gone a short distance from the
court house when an officer ran out to call Dick
back. Well, well, what now. He was taken to
the judge, who turned and asked him his name

and that of his mother before her marriage.
Dick replied that his mother's name had been
Nancy Johns. "My God," said the judge, "is
this the son of my little school playmate Nancy
Johns?" It was. Well, he would be busy that
day but on the morrow Dick must come and dine
with him and spend the day with him. Next day
Dick strode up the hill to Judge Price's mansion
house, dressed in good style. He was ushered in
and soon the judge appeared and told Dick that
he was once Sir Rose Price and had a large estate in the west of Cornwall, but had left there
many years before. Dick then knew it all, but
kept mum. Soon they were riding in the carriage
and four with postilions. After a long drive
they came back to dinner and he had a very pleasant visit with the judge.

Now this Judge Price ran away from England when a young man and left the estate go to
ruin in the hands of strangers. He had a step-
sister, and they fell in love with each other.
They applied to the Bishop for leave to marry,
but of course were refused. They left in a hurry
and it was not known where they went. Of
course they hired some ship to convey them

secretly to far off Australia, where his superior education procured for him some high positions until he became judge of one of the government high courts. He never returned to his estate and I think it escheated to the Crown.

But Dick had not made that fortune for Mary, so in the spring of 1855 he found himself in San Francisco, California. He converted his money into English sovereigns and took ship for London. He had neglected writing home for a long time. They sailed down the Pacific coast of South America, but got shipwrecked on the coast of Peru. They lost everything but their lives and had a hard time to save them. Money all gone down in the trunk, tools all gone, in a strange country where he could not understand the language. What next?

Peru and Chili were at war. There was a chance to join the Peruvian navy, as they wanted men, especially officers. He joined and went on board. A first-class petty officer, he soon learned some of the language. One day while lying in the harbor of Callaio, in came a Chillian frigate, with colors flying and guns ran out of portholes, cast anchor and challenged to fight. All hands

were piped to quarters and guns double shotted
on the Peruvian. Just then a large English three
decker man-of-war which was lying there with
steam up, slipped her cable, and steamed in between the two beligerents. No fighting inside
the headlands—contrary to the law of nations.
Dick said, "Oh, how I wanted the Chillian to let
fly at one side and our ship at the other." Oh,
such arrogance. The Chillian, after night came,
went to sea. Next morning they went out to
hunt her, but she had gone home, so they had no
fight.

A few days after that Dick went on shore
with a number of other officers to attend a ball,
all dressed in his naval uniform. A little urchin
stepped up to him and said, "I know you; your
name is Mr. Trevellick." ":Yes," said Dick,
"but what is yours!" "My name is Joe." "Yes,
but what besides Joe?" "Joe Hartley," he answered. He said he was there in a vessel from
Scilly, Wm. Lakey captain. The next morning
a boat fully manned left the side of the Peruvian
frigate with our hero in full uniform in the stern.
Soon greetings were had, cigars passed around,
men treated to grog, and a good chat about home

and old friends, and of Dick's adventures. Good-byes were spoken and flags dipped in honor of the man-of-war's men.

But soon the war ended and Dick was paid off. He then went to Panama late in 1855 and entered the service of the Pacific Mail Steamship Company, visiting nearly all the ports on the American shore of the Pacific. He afterwards was sent to Aspinwall to assist in the construction of the mail and steamship wharves.

CHAPTER IV.

IN 1857 he was working along the Gulf of Mexico at his trade, and in New Orleans he was elected as president of the Shipcarpenters and Caulkers' Union, when they secured the nine-hour system largely through his agitation.

One day while his brother Sam was working in a shipyard in New York, some one called him by name, and another young man standing by asked Sam if he had a brother in New Orleans. He knew a man there named Richard Trevellick, a shipcarpenter and president of the Union, and also president of a temperance society. Sam replied that it surely was him, but he had thought him dead. That evening Sam wrote him a letter. As soon as he found that Sam was in New York, he decided to go there, but he had that day signed articles to go to London. He saw the captain and told him he was going to New York, but the captain insisted that he should go with him to

London. However, they soon found another man to take his place, but had to pay him a good bonus. Dick left on the next steamer for New York.

On arriving there a cordial welcome by the brother and family and the writer of this narrative awaited him. We had not seen him for nearly ten years. He soon found that Mary had got tired of waiting for him and had been married to a butcher. Another set-back for our sun-tanned hero.

He soon got work on the Marine Railway at Red Hook point, South Brooklyn. In less than two weeks he had to keep the men's time and in a short time was foreman, during which time he was a member of the Shipcarpenters Union of New York and vicinity. When winter set in he took Sam back to New Orleans with him. They worked there during the winter, but when the hot weather came on Sam was afraid of Yellow fever and returned to New York to his wife.

Soon after Dick went up to Franklin in charge of a gang of 12 men, to repair a steamboat, and while there got sick himself. When he got better he told the lady of the house, where he

had been kindly cared for, that he did not know
how he could pay her unless he married one of the
daughters. Well, we will draw the veil there,
but the result was that he married Miss Victoria,
whom he always called "my Vic." when speaking
of her to me. She bore him five children, one of
whom is dead. The others are all holding their
own in this country.

Dick soon went on a steamer and was running on the Mississippi and tributaries when the
war broke out. One day a Confederate committee
waited on him and told him he must be an officer
on one of the gun-boats they were then fitting
out. But he flatly refused to bear arms against
freedom. Shortly after, another committe told
him to join the army or leave the country. He
decided to leave. He went to the British Consul
and demanded a pass through the Confederate
lines, as he was not then a full American citizen.
He got the pass and went home and told his wife
to take her choice: Stay with her own family—
some of whom were in the Confederate service—
or go North with him. She chose to share his
love and fortunes. A broker was seen, furniture

sold at a great sacrifice, and that night found
them on a steamer bound up river.

They arrived opposite Fort Donaldson and
were detained by Southern officers in charge.
The British pass was disregarded. After a day
or two the news came that the Union forces were
coming to capture the fort. if they could. The
passengers were allowed to go on up the Ohio
as best they could. There was no room for non-
combatants. Dick arrived at Pittsburgh and
wrote to his brother in New York, and soon he
was on his way there with his new Southern
wife.

But it was no use repining; duty now called
on him for extra exertion. He had now to provide for the life partner of his joys and sorrows
and for his now fast approaching family, so he
determined to take Horace Greeley's advice to go
west and grow up with the country. While he
might never again behold that beautiful land in
which he was born, he might not hear again the
sweet notes of the cuckoo or the skylark, he
might not smell the fragrance of the furze and
the heather of his native isle or eat of the fruit
cultivated by his father's hand, he might not

gather the shellfish from his native rocks, or dig
up the sand eels from the sand on the ocean shore,
or see the great waves as they rolled home from
the great Atlantic and broke in fury on his native
strand; still, in this vast expanse of country of
which he now became a citizen, there were a
thousand blessings in store for the willing and
skillful hands of the laborer and mechanic. He
could ride through the primeval forests and see
the vast, powerful machinery, cutting timber
wherewith to build homes and shelter for man and
beast; he could sail out on the great lakes and
see the great inland marine ships carrying the
fruits of the farm and the products of the mine
to be put to the use of man; he could hear the
shrill whistle of the locomotive as it scampered
away over the almost boundless prairies of the
great West, gathering up the cattle and grain
and transporting them away to the seaboard; he
could see the great fields of waving wheat and of
ripening corn; he could hear the loud roar of
Niagara and the sweet notes of the mocking bird
and the oriole.

But he could also see that notwithstand-
ingall those bountiful provisions of nature,

and all those beautiful surroundings still the
workers that were developing those great resources of his now adopted home were poor.
There was excessive toil, there was poverty, and
crime in abundance. The sharp, shrewd specu-
lator gathered up the fruits of the laborer's toil
through usury, extortion and by taking advantage of the necessities of the poor. Machinery
was being invented by the brain of the mechanic
and inventor, but they seldom got any of the profits accruing from those improvements.

He determined now to put those talents of
memory and oratory to the education of the toiling masses, among whom he had cast his lot.
With that end in view he went on to that fast
developing, thriving city of Detroit. He started
to make his permanent home there, and there he
lived, and, after rearing his family to maturity,
went down to the grave lamented by many of his
followers.

On arriving at Detroit he obtained employment at the great yard of the Dry Dock Company, joining Shipcarpenters' and Caulkers'
Union No. 4 of Detroit, of which he was soon
after elected president. In 1865 he was elected

president of the Shipcarpenters' and Caulkers'
International Union, and something took place
then that changed his manner of life.   A strike
had taken place in the ship docks and yards of
Buffalo, and the Detroit unions were asked to
render financial assistance.   They did, but could
only send small sums.   The express companies'
agents had divulged the secret of the amounts
sent down and the employers laughed at the
futile attempts to hold out, and thought to starve
them into submission.   Dick then took another
method.   He advised all unions sending money to
designate larger amounts: for instance, if they
sent $30 to pay for sending $300.   That worked
all right, and the bosses looked blue.   The en-
velopes containing the money were sealed before
they left the hands of the secretaries.

One day a Detroit ship put into Buffalo for
repairs, but the men would not work on her.
The captain wrote to Trevellick's boss to send
down some men from there to do the work, so
the boss went to Canada and secretly sent five
men from there.   But Dick discovered the trick
and checkmated it by telegraphing to the Buffalo
union to meet the men and buy them off and send

them back home.   They did so, and the captain
was mad.   He wrote to Detroit and told the result.   Dick's boss came to him and said, "I think
you must have been interfering in my business in
preventing those men from working on that
vessel in Buffalo."   Dick told him he had, as
that was his duty, he being presiding officer of
the unions.   "Well," said the boss, "you may
consider yourself discharged."   "All right, sir,
but you will soon send for me to come back."
Oh, no, he wouldn't.

Well, that evening Dick called a meeting of
the local union and told his story.   A strike was
voted at once, and next day all the men were idle.
There were five ships on the docks, and the
owners tried to get the men to work, but in vain,
until Dick was taken back.   A meeting of the
owners and bosses was had and they insisted that
Dick's boss must take him back or forfeit $500
per day for detention of the ships.   That brought
him to time and he sent for Dick to come back.

Next morning all the men were at work and
Dick was among them.   He was making a ship's
rudder, which requires a good workman.   About
nine o'clock out came the boss.

"Well, you are here, I see."

"Yes, and you sent for me."

"Well, now, I hope this won't occur again," said the boss.

Dick answered, "I know it will not, as I shall now discharge myself, and you can't have the pleasure of doing so."

The boss expostulated and begged him to stay, but no, that spirit of resistance had gotten control, and Dick worked no more with the tools.

From that day on the active life of Dick in labor's cause commenced. Henceforth he would tell the Americans what Pliny told the Romans— that "great estates have ruined empires." He became too perceptive of what was going on around him to miss the truth of Mills' remark that the cunning and ingenuity of man had reached the ideal in methods of production, and that the problem for statesmen and political economists was, "How can we best secure equitable distribution?" To carry the discussion of this question into the public halls and the workshops was the task he set out to accomplish.

About this time he was selected by the De-

troit Trades' Assembly, of which he was presi-
dent, to represent it at a convention of presidents
of all international unions, held at Louisville.
Among those present were Andrew C. Cameron,
editor of Workingmen's Advocate of Chicago;
John Whitten, of Massachusetts; Thomas C.
Knowles, of New York; John Busby, of Indiana;
Robert Schilling, of Milwaukee; Wm. H. Sylves,
of the Moulders' Union; Boucher, of the Printers'
Union; Siney of the Miners' Union; Wm. Bailey,
of Missouri; George Bigler, of Kentucky; Thomas
Armstrong, of Pennsylvania; and Trevellick, of
Detroit, Michigan. He kept a photographic
group of those men in his house as long as he
lived.

After a five days' session they adjourned to
meet in Baltimore the next year, at which meeting all trades were represented—65 delegates
were present. The next year they met in Chicago. The Chicago Trades' Assembly took
quite a fancy to Dick and made him an offer that
if he would move there they would buy a lot and
build him a house, and that they would give him
a salary and constitute themselves into a lecture
bureau and collect the proceeds of the lectures

(principally on the eight hour system and labor and finance.)   They met one Sunday with him present to decide on a salary.   Most of them favored $1,000, but one man arose and objected to the whole proceeding.   He thought Dick was no better to work for a living in a shipyard than himself.   Dick then arose and heartily thanked the assembly for the generous offer, but positively refused to accept the position.   He said if the objection had come from any other trade than his own—that trade that had always been at the front of labor reform, but had produced so few men that could stand up before a public audience and discuss problems of political economy—he would have overlooked it, but not now.   He told them he should return to his own city, and did so.

That objector, unfortunately, was Frank Lawlor, now deceased, who in after years, with the votes of Democrats and those of his own nationality, was sent to Congress, and at last brought up in the world-renowned common council of Chicago, where he showed many traits of independence and honesty.

But while Frank went to Congress, Dick was framing platforms and nominating governors and presidents.   Both died poor men, but their loss is regretted by the workingmen.

Dick marched in front of the first great torchlight eight-hour procession in Chicago. He was guarded by 20 policemen, as his life was considered in danger at that time.   I spent the next day with him in Chicago.   In the evening we attended church in one of the large churches on Wabash avenue.   The minister preached a fine, flowery sermon, full of rhetoric, etc.   At the close he prayed that God would bless the nation and the governing powers and that he would especially bless the poor and grant them patience and fortitude to bear with their humble lot.

"Yea, Lord, and give them bread," said Dick, with his head bowed on the front seat.

Every head was raised to see where that sound came from.   The minister closed the prayer abruptly, the benediction was pronounced, and we came out.   He said afterwards that he hated to see and hear so much cant and hypocrisy in the churches.   That was not the way Christ taught his disciples to preach the doctrines of Christianity.   He told them to preach to the poor, the halt, the maimed and the blind.

The following first of May he led the great eight-hour procession through Chicago streets to Harmon Court.   Mayor Rice was president of the day.   Wilbur F. Story of the Times was hung in effigy on a printers' wagon in the procession. Dick made a grand speech and was cheered to the echo.   Many men cried out: "Trevellick for next president of the United States;" but they were ignorant of his nationality.

Dick often quoted some passage of Scripture as a text for his lecture.   On one occasion when on a visit to our city of Joliet, through the kindness of Rev. Laing he delivered a fine address in the Universalist church on the sacredness of the Christian Sabbath and the duty of the workers especially to observe it and refrain from labor or debauch on that day.

He could use great eloquence at times.   About four years ago on Labor Day in Joliet he led a procession of trades unions in a carriage with Mayor Haley, and afterward spoke at the park with such eloquence and sound arguments that he electrified both men and women.   One lady exclaimed in an audible voice, "Oh, I do dearly love that man."   She was a perfect stranger to him and a married woman, too.   But such is the power of oratory.

The writer of this narrative never knew Dick to show high temper but once.   In the Workingmen's Advocate office of Chicago a discussion took place as to who wrote the platform of the first National Labor Congress.   Dick said he composed and wrote it, and one of the men present called him a liar.   That fired him.   He arose quickly and approached the man with his fists clinched, and demanded that he take that back. When he saw that eagle eye and widely distended nostrils and scowling brow he took it back quickly and apologized, and said he must have been misinformed.   But Dick wrote that memorable platform, as will be shown hereafter.

The spring following the Baltimore convention and before the meeting in Chicago, Dick issued a call for a state convention, which met at Ionia, Michigan, and was well attended.   On the 12th of December, 1868, was printed at Grand Rapids the platform of principles on which the National Labor Union and Industrial Brotherhood stood, and which is substantially the declaration of principles on which the Knights of Labor

stood after that.   Some planks of that platform
are included in all Labor party, Greenback, Populist and Farmers' Alliance platforms since that
time—notably the Omaha and Ocala platforms.
Dick was elected president of the National Labor
Union in 1871 and re-elected in 1872 and 1873.

During 1874 and 1875 he helped to form the
Greenback party, and drew most of his inspira-
tion on that question from that Grand Old Friend
and adviser of President Lincoln—Alexander
Campbell, of La Salle, Ill., who was thoroughly
posted on the currency and financial questions of
that day.   Dick was not long in perceiving that
money is a measure of value and an institution of
law, designed to measure the numerical relation
of value and accordingly took his place in the
ranks of Greenback agitators, whose special mission was to agitate reform on the currency question, and to proclaim that the greenback was not
a representative of money, but was and is money
itself, and that a nation is actually poorer in proportion to the amount of the precious metals she
diverts from their proper uses and holds in the
shape of coined money.

In 1876 he was a delegate to the convention

that nominated the Peter Cooper and Sam Casey ticket, and was president of the Greenback State Convention held at Grand Rapids.   In 1880 he presided over that memorable convention in Chicago which nominated General Weaver for President, and there Dick showed great powers of mind and physical endurance.   There were so many factions of reformers, all striving for the mastery and recognition of their ideas, that they were very hard to control, and there his wonderful memory and masterly energy carried him through the trying ordeal.

The temporary chairman, Rev. De La Matyr, had entirely succumbed when Dick took the chair. After four hours of active ruling, Judge Stubbs, of Iowa, a fine robust and dignified old gentleman, tried to give Dick a rest, but he gave in in half an hour.   Dick then ran it until about 8 o'clock in the evening, when Terrell, of Texas, took control, but he, too, soon got things badly mixed and gave up in disgust.   Dick then took the gavel, and stood there like a rock all night, until 6 in the morning—when the ticket was perfected— and was highly praised for his powers of endurance and fair rulings.

At the Greenback State Convention held in Detroit, which convention nominated good-hearted old Josiah Begole for governor, Dick again presided..

He lectured several times in Joliet on Land, on Labor and . on Finance. He made many speeches in this congressional district to the miners, and gave them good advice and encouragement. When his old friend-A. Campbell ran for congress in this district Dick made many speeches to the farmers, miners and mechanics with good results, and electdd his man, who, in company with Wm. (Pig-Iron) Kelly, of Pennsylvania, uncovered the plot of the money powers of America and England to demonetize silver, and published the plot and its results to the world.

For over 20 years Dick kept up the agitation on the rights of labor and the rights of man, visiting many places and speaking in almost every state and territory in the United States. When the eight-hour committee was casting about for a champion to carry their grievances to Congress, Dick was the man elected, and he did more to procure the passage of the measure than any other living person.

He was in Washington at that time nearly four months, mostly at his own expense, which crippled him financially. He was there again just before General Grant's second election, urging on the heads of departments to pay the navy yard workmen the wages that had been kept back from them on account of the shortened day. He accomplished his purpose then, and the men were ordered paid. He urged on Naval Secretary Thompson to do justice to the men under his control at the yards and arsenals of the United States.

Again he took an active part in procuring the adoption of the eight-hour system for the letter carriers. While T. V. Powderly was adverse to pushing the system as premature, and advised the further education of the masses, Trevellick thought by adopting the system as soon as possible the men would have more time to improve their minds. But since that the system is making rapid strides under the auspices of the Federation of Labor. Knights of Labor and kindred other organizations in the United States, and the labor unions of Brittain and other countries of Europe are agitating the matter there with every prospect of success.

Mr. Trevellick was an honorary member of seven trades unions, and he was probably the only man in America ever elected to honorary membership in a typographical union who has never in any way been connected with the trade.

The confidence reposed in him by the organized work people of the United States is evidenced by the fact that they subscribed quite a sum of money towards building him a beautiful home.

CHAPTER V.

WHEN T. V. Powderly issued the call to the workingmen for funds to build the home for Dick, he used the following words: "After Trevellick's death scores of men will be running over this country collecting money to build monuments to Trevellick. Let us build the monument in giving him a home in his old age." Again, in sending his part of the subscription to the committee, he sent the following unique letter which was full of truth:

"I overheard a conversation between two men to-day, one endeavoring to persuade the other to go with him to take a drink. They were standing in front of a saloon kept by a friend of both. One said: 'I have stood at Harry's bar ten times a week for the last five years, and I never took a shingle off his roof yet.' Counting up the number of drinks taken by this man at that bar for five years, and averaging them at five cents a

drink, he must have spent at the lowest calcula-
tion $130. He is not a drunkard; he would have
felt insulted even if I had told him he was re-
garded as a moderate drinker. I, too, have passed
that same bar for the last five years about ten
times a week, but I have never stood at the bar;
consequently I have saved by not doing so just
$130. The men whose conversation I overheard
were workingmen. In one county in this state
$17,000,000 was spent in one year for drink—
$17,000,000 devoted to tearing down happy homes
and putting shingles on the roofs of idlers. My
thoughts traveled back to the time when the Trevellick home fund was started and I felt a tinge
of shame pass over me and said to myself, The
workingmen of the United States and Canada
have raised in two years the sum of $1,200 for the
purpose of giving to one of labor's bravest defenders—to a man who has sacrificed twenty
homes in the cause of shackled labor, and the
workingmen of one county in my native state have
helped to swell the sum spent in tearing down
homes to $17,000,000. If Richard F. Trevellick
had started in the saloon business ten years ago
he would have been a millionaire to-day. He

would have had workingmen putting shingles on
his house all of these years. His work has been
in the opposite direction. He has been engaged
not only in putting shingles on the roofs of workingmen's houses, but he has been busy night and
day teaching them that to every man belongs the
right of having a home of his own, to every man
belongs the right to own the fruits of his labor.
How has he been recompensed? Can anything
we may do recompense him for his years of toil?
I do not think we can ever pay him, but we can
do a little towards it. I have never placed a
shingle on the roof of a saloon keeper. I ask
those who have been engaged doing so to stop it
at least for a time and help to put a few shingles
on the roof of a friend. I value every shingle on
the roof of Trevellick's house at five dollars. I
contribute my mite to buy one shingle. I ask of
the workingmen of America to help pay for all of
these shingles. If you cannot pay for a whole
shingle, then co-operate with your neighbors in
doing it. Let us make a vigorous effort to have
all the shingles paid for. Who will buy the next
shingle?

T. V. POWDERLY."

Trevellick's father was a strong temperance advocate, and lectured on that subject at times. He hoped to see the day that intoxicating liquors should be sold from the shelves of the druggist only by the prescription of a physician. So it was natural that his son should be taught the evils of intemperance by him. Another thing that instilled into Dick's mind temperance principles was the great wave of temperance or teetotalism excitement that swept over the west of England about the time of Dick's apprenticeship. The teachings in his Sunday School and Methodist church, of which he was a frequent attendant, all helped to determine the habits of his after life. He was an officer of several temperance organizations (as were also his brothers) and could deliver a good lecture on that subject, as was shown in our own city of Joliet. Oh, how he grieved to see the hard working man taking the money from his wife and family and home and maintaining the idle in affluence and wealth. He was over 25 before he knew the taste of liquor, and only then as a medicine on shipboard where no other stimulant could be procured. In after life he seldom drank anything that would over-

stimulate or weaken the intellect. He would say
the workers had no·more sense than they needed
to compete with the sharper that was fleecing
them. When the temperance organizations tried
to amend the Nebraska constitution he made a
thorough canvass of that state and made the acquaintance of most of the temperance advocates
af the country, both ladies and gentlemen.

He was also a strong believer in woman's
suffrage. He stumped the state of Colorado on
that issue. He argued that it was her inherent
right if she was an American citizen and entitled
to life, liberty and the pursuit of happiness. She
should have the right to vote for the assessor of
her taxes and the judge who probated her estate
or who might possibly try her son for alleged
crime, or marry her daughter, perhaps, to a man
whom she knew to be an unworthy subject for
her son-in-law. He claimed that a woman's
property should not be taxed without representation. It was in violation of the spirit of the
declaration of principles and of the Constitution
of the United States.

As will be seen in the latter part of this
work, he was a strong advocate of the principles

enunciated in the platforms of the People's or
third party.   He was bitterly opposed to contract
or convict labor, when it interfered with the free
labor of the American law-abiding citizen.   He
was adverse to the system now in vogue, of doing
work by contract instead of by the day.   He said
it looked like a stigma against the honesty and
integrity of the American workman, and it too
often led to loss by the contractor or loss of wages
to the workman; either that, bad workmanship
or inferior material.

Mr. Trevellick was very outspoken in giving
his convictions on a subject.   He would speak the
truth without fear.   It was sometimes hard for
members to bear.   On one occasion in our city he
was invited to advise an organization of combined
builders and their employes.   He told them
flatly he did not think they could co-operate
together successfully very long as their interests
were opposed to each other, especially as the
bosses were taking most of the work by contract.
Of course it was to their interest to get the work
done as cheaply as possible, both for themselves
and the owner of the building, while the workmen would want to make all the wages they

could. It would require much forbearance to harmonize. But the worst danger was in having traitors in their own ranks. If there were 70 members it was safe to assume that there were three or four among the number, as Christ had one out of twelve. It was as he predicted. The society soon collapsed.

Another time, at the close of the war, he was invited to address the Legislature of Louisiana on the best method of reconstruction of the southern state governments. He told them very plainly that they would have to rely more on their own exertions and teach their sons and daughters to do some of the hard work and duties of life. They had been too long training in idleness and luxury at the expense of the cheap and hard labor of the slave. They would have to do justice to the laborer and pay him for his toil. They would have to be more enterprising and engage in developing the products of the mine and factory and train themselves to work instead of practicing too much on each other with the bowie knife and the revolver. Some of his audience took it as a great insult to Southern chivalry, and on coming out of the hall a friend persuaded him to get out of harm's way immediately.   He did so, and another gentlemen that was on the rostrum was waylaid by two men, but they saw their mistake in time and one said to the other:

"We have got the wrong man.   This is not Trevellick."

He was warned many times by the working-man to be on his guard while advocating the eight-hour system in manufacturing centres, but he was no coward.

CHAPTER VI.

TREVELLICK was almost as cosmopolitan in religion as he was in regard to nationality. His religion was to do good to all persons without regard to their nationality, color or creed. He was not a bigot in any sense of the word. He firmly believed in the constitutional right of every person worshipping God according to the dictates of their own consciences. He knew well that a man's religious belief is created by the teachings of his early youth, and by his observations and the education and circumstances surrounding him. If we were born in India we might be Buddhists, if in Turkey we might be Mohammedans, if in Utah we might be Mormons, of if in Ireland or Spain we might be Catholics. But if he could prove by reason and sound argument that one religion was better for the human race than another he would be likely to do as St. Paul said: "Knowing these things we persuade men."

On one of his visits to our city we attended church in the evening, and after returning to the house of his friend, Fire Marshal Ryan, as he sat in the chair discussing the merits of the sermon, he raised his eyes towards the ceiling and proceeded to repeat the Lord's Prayer in a slow and reverent manner. He seemed like one inspired as he began: "Our Father who art in heaven; hallowed be Thy name; Thy kingdom come; Thy will be done on earth as it is in heaven." He stopped there and exclaimed:"Oh! if I have been or can be instrumental in having God's will done on earth,as it is in heaven, then I shall have accomplished my mission."

He believed in the Fatherhood of God and the brotherhood of man. The world was his country and the religious teaching of Christ was his creed His was a mission of peace, sobriety, industry and love to his fellowman. The world had many heroes, as Washington, Lincoln, Grant, Sherman and Sheridan on this continent; Bolivar and Gomez and others in South America; England had her Wellington, her Nelson, her Havelock and her Gordon; France had her Bonaparte, Italy her Garabaldi, Austria her Kossuth and

Poland her Kosiusko; but all their escutcheons were smeared with human blood. Trevellick believed in governing like Christ—by sheathing the sword and conquering his enemies by kindness, conciliation and arbitration.

His firmness under strong temptation was exemplified on many occasions, but on none more so than at one time in his own home. Two gentlemen were seeking to be elected United States Senator from Michigan. One was a friend of the producing and laboring classes; the other was inclined to favor corporate power and the concentration of wealth. It was necessary, of course, to elect members of the legislature favorable to one or the other. One night, after he had retired, he heard a ring at the door. He opened it and in walked two gentlemen. They wished to see him on special business and required a fire and a light. These were procured, and they then told him that their business was to get him to take the stump for their friend, the concentration man, for senator. He argued that it would be entirely against the principles he had always advocated. They begged and expostulated with him for several hours, but he still refused. When they rose to go, one said:

"We see that arguments are in vain. Now we will try what money will do. We will give you $300 per lecture for 10 lectures, we fixing the time and place."

He replied: "Gentlemen, your offer is exceedingly liberal, but you cannot buy my integrity. Good night."

When he went up-stairs his wife wanted to know about the matter, and he told her.

"Oh!" she exclaimed, "what a nice thing that $3000 would be to educate our children."

He said it staggered him for a moment, but he soon replied, "Vic, our children will be educated, and not at the expense of their father's disgrace."

On another occasion, while on a visit to my house, he received a letter from the mayor of Detroit asking him to come home quickly as they wanted to run him for the legislature on a Republican ticket. His election was certain. He wrote a reply and showed it to me. It was, as near as I can remember, as follows:

"Sir:—I thank you for your kind offer, but I must decline. I have started out on a career to try to educate my fellow workmen all over the country to think and act intelligently, and were I to accept an office at the hands of one of the large parties I should have to be too much under the control of that party organization. If I shall succeed, at the end of five years, in establishing a party of the laboring and producing classes, then if they should wish to elect me to some lucrative office I should be at their services."

His purposes and aims were not well understood, by reason of the prejudice engendered against him. The name of Labor Agitator was as bad as mad dog. The refined and educated readers of the large daily papers and magazines thought that his teachings were anarchistic, but they were not, as I shall hereafter show.

A little incident in our city will show the effect of prejudice and the timidity of capitalists. On one of his visits here his friend, Mr. Ryan, took him to see the Athenaeum, at the rolling mills. Mr. Crane, the manager, showed them all the facilities for physical and mental development that had been provided by the company for the amusement and instruction of the workmen and their families—the library, reading room, billiard room, gymnasium, baths, lecture room, night school, day school for any of their children who might wish to attend, etc.

On his return home to my house, he expressed a strong desire to speak in the building to the workmen and urge them to take advantage of those privileges which were at their command. On his next visit we organized a committee and went to see the trustees. They were afraid to assume the responsibility of allowing a *Labor Agitator* to lecture in the hall, and referred us to the manager. After seeing him twice or thrice he refused to let him lecture there. But Dick wanted to show the men how they should appreciate the efforts of the employers to provide for their edification and amusement, and pride themselves on having the best kind of an institution of any mill in the country at that time. (I may be pardoned for saying here that the workmen do not patronize the institution as much as they might or as the officials of the company would like to see.)

The lectures, debates and papers read there

at the Smoking Conference are models of rhetoric,
logic and Christian instruction, being conducted
by ministers, lawyers, and other professional
men, as well as the employers and employes.
How Dick would glory in taking part in these
exercises! But he is gone. May his good works
bear fruit for the benefit of the toilers of the
world, is the prayer of the writer.

Trevellick wanted to see his fellow workmen
in this, the land of his adoption, the model workmen of the world—here where they had the privilege of electing their own rulers and of sending
men to make the laws for their own government,
where there are free schools and free religious instruction, a healthy climate and a fertile country
with boundless resources.   He wished for them
to have good homes, surrounded with flower and
vegetable gardens; he wanted them to have more
time to enjoy themselves and in getting that education that would lift them to a higher plane of
good citizenship; he wish to see them dressed in
good, decent clothes, going to their churches instead of to the grogshop.   Too well he knew that
a man working incessantly for ten hours per day
and then having to go three or four miles to get

to and from his work could not feel much like
taking part in any mental developments; he would
see more mirth and hilarity at Tom, Dick or
Harry's card table or saloon, and he would go
there, where all the allurements are held out.
Dick knew that the shortening of the hours of
toil and the adoption of good laws in New Zealand
had produced the best kind of results.   They now
boast of having the best government in the world.

Trevellick was not long in perceiving that
the money power of the country was governing
the votes and actions of both of the large political
parties, and it made him anxious to build up a
party that would be represented in the caucuses
and conventions by more of the working and producing classes, so he was ready to join any friends
of labor in accomplishing that end.   When the
Labor party nominated a ticket with David Davis
for President and Joel Parker for Vice-President,
Dick took a prominent part in the nomination, and
was sent at the head of a committee to try to get
the Democrats to indorse the ticket.

On arriving at Cincinnati they attended a
meeting of the Democratic Central Committee
and stated their request.   A delegate from New

York arose and objected to indorsing the ticket.
He said he represented August Belmont and that
the Democrats should never be disgraced by hav-
a workingman's candidate at the head of their
ticket. Trevellick asked him to withdraw the
language, but he would not, and again repeated
it. Trevellick then told him that no matter who
they—the Democrats—nominated that he should
be defeated as sure as the sun rises and sets. Of
course they laughed him to derision, and went on
and nominated Horace Greely. The Labor Committee then sent Dick down to canvass Pennsylvania for Grant on the tariff issue. He went all
through and spoke and organized clubs in all the
large cities, and it made a great furor. Pennsylvania voted Republican by an overwhelming majority, and "as goes Pennsylvania so goes the
Union."

Trevellick advocated protection to infant industries until they could compete in the markets
of the world, and all necessities that we could not
procure in this country should come in free. He
argued that if the American capitalist would be
content to take the same rates of profits on the
capital invested as the English investor, that the

United States could compete in the markets of the
world with them, notwithstanding the higher
rates of wages paid here.   Our machinery and the
ability to procure the raw material at less cost
would more than cover the loss of the extra wages
in developing the resources of the country.

CHAPTER VII.

TO illustrate more fully Mr. Trevellick's views and ideas, in stronger and better language than I might use, I take the liberty of quoting from an article published in the Galveston News, about the time of the great south-western railroad strike on the Gould system. The writer of the article says:

"'No man,'' says Quintilian, "according to my definition, can be a perfect orator unless he is a good man.' If intensity and earnestness of purpose; if genuine love and sympathy; if life-long devotion to the cause that seeks by industrial emancipation to lessen the sorrows of the human race, could proclaim man's perfection in oratory, then, surely, but few men would stand higher in the estimation of his countrymen, as an orator, than Richard F. Trevellick, who with defiant hopefulness and unyielding energy has taught to man universal brotherhood and the conditions

which make it possible. The reasonableness of
the hope that is in a man, and the fervor and intensity with which he sets it forth, constitute the
chief qualities upon which reliance is to be placed
in the endeavor to lead men from the slough of
despondency and a sluggish apathy, born of oppression, into the full glare of the noonday sun.
How well and mightily has Trevellick contributed
to set the battle in array, let attest the univer-
sality of discussion upon topics connected with
the equitable distribution of wealth and the justice of the demand of labor. Ever steadfast and
never wavering, he has borne aloft the flag when
the deferment of hope and success had dampened
the ardor and appalled the hearts of the stoutest.
By his dignity and commanding presence he ar-
rests attention; by his force and earnestness he
compels confidence; with his fund of anecdote and
illustration, culled from a traveler's experience in
the four quarters of the globe, he interests; and
by his argument he arouses thought or carries
conviction to his hearers.''

In the early days of his appearance on the
platform as a champion of labor, Trevellick's
keenness of perception in social and industrial

affairs led him to discern the sagacity of the warning given by Edmund Burke when he said to the
English Parliament, in reference to the taxing of
the American colonies: "We are shearing not a
sheep but a wolf."

At the outset of his career, as one who
preached the doctrine that the laborer is worthy
of his hire, and that, in the language of Adam
Smith, the produce of labor constitutes the natural recompense or wages of labor, Trevellick
warned his capitalistic hearers of the reign of. law
in the domain of the social as well as the physical
world. He said:

"That which a man soweth shall he also
reap. The sins of a man may be hidden to the
world, awaiting the occasion of the resurrection,
but sooner or later comes the resurrection, and
with the resurrection comes the judgment. Eternal and immutable are the principles of morality
for it is not given unto men to escape the consequences of their actions. Action and reaction are
equal and opposite. They strike the equation.
What tho' justice be leaden-heeled and delayeth
her coming, yet shall she surely come, and shall
deal out to each according to the deeds done in

the body.   What is done has already blended itself with the boundless, ever-living, ever-working
universe, and will also work there for good or
evil, openly or secretly, throughout all time."

But all unheeded has been the warning. The
pleasant optimism of a deductive political economy, voiced by Bastiat in his celebrated doctrine:
"In proportion to the increase of capital the absolute share (of a given product) falling to capital
augmented, but the relative share is diminished.
On the other hand, the share falling to labor is
increased, both absolutely and relatively," has
not been realized in the present generation of men.

On the apriori principles of Mr. Herbert
Spencer's evolutionary philosophy, we may, indeed, trace out the pathway along which it is
hoped to arrive at the Millennium, in which evil
as a factor will be removed from the government
of the world; but such flights of the imagination
are purely within the realms of metaphysical
speculation, and can afford neither guidance nor
comfort to a civilization .that travels upon its
stomach, and which at every moment is compelled
to adapt itself to the ever-present yet ever-chang-
ing environments.

The exigences of the moment press upon the administrator, or legislator, with an impervious necessity that compels to instant action. However well versed in the abstract theories of government, however desirous of applying principles carefully elaborated by logical method from facts furnished from the everyday life of a tugging, bustling, over-reaching world, yet is he continually called upon amidst the clamor of faction, the strife of party or the cries of the distressed whose necessities demand immediate relief. To formulate a plan of action which his reflective judgment or more mature deliberation would never sanction, and which in its ultimate consequences, may bring about results little dreamed of at the moment of its inception.

A quarter of a century ago when Trevellick appeared on the platform with the doctrine that slavery was not alone determined by the color and texture of a man's skin, there were none to do him reverence and but few to give him audience. These things, they said, are for the consideration of those who groan beneath the yoke of king craft and priestcraft, and not for us, firm in the faith that a government of the people by the

people and for the people, shall not perish from
the face of the earth.   "Life, liberty and the pursuit of happiness," and the usual stock quotations
were brought forward and spread to the public
gaze, and the cause of Liberty was considered as
stoutly vindicated.   But the fundamental princi-
pals of human nature have not perceptibly
changed throughout historic ages.   "They were
even as we are," says an old philosopher; and
the philosophy of the optimistic school that posits
profound psychic change as a necessary cause of
the increasing amenities and culture of social life,
is the error of those who mistake a rhythm of
movement for a refashioning of the human soul at
the hands of the Infinite.   The true grandeur of
a man consists in his moral, not in his intellectual
life, save as this may minister to and give strengh
to the former.   On the supposition of uniform
moral regeneration, how shall we account for
the assertion of a keenly observant writer on the
condition of London's poor, that below the level
of the respectable artisan class, the tendency is
downward; downward to an ineffable degradation;
downward to a point where the mind of the observer is irresistibly led to speculate on the doc-

trine of "moral idiocy." It is long .since that
Professor Huxley declared that the life of London's poor was worse than the South African
savage.

"My ideal of life," said Wendell Phillips,
"would be that of the New England village of
fifty years ago." The New England village of
fifty years ago is the great city of to-day. Is
there lacking within its limits any show of poverty, any phase of sorrow, any species of crime,
any kind of vice or exhibition of human degreda-
tion to be found within the walls of any European
city? Circe walks in the shadows of the twilight,
and her daughters are numerous; the highway-
man and the burglar keep pace with the mechanic
in the ingenuity of means wherewith to ply their
arts; our leading reviews discuss such questions
as, "Are we a nation of rascals?"

In Trevellick's own city of Detroit are to be
seen men who have accumulated ten or fifteen
millions of dollars in but a few years, and who,
beyond the mere superintendence in some subor-
dinate department or of quasi general management in the counting house, have given nothing
to society that it could not willingly let die.

"Give me," says Garfield, "the financial records of a nation, and I will write its history." He doubtless would have assumed by a process of deductive reasoning that the "Iron Law" of the German economists, or the law that the share of the laborer is that part of the product upon which he will consent to live and propagate his species, must regulate the lives and habits of the vast majority of its citizens where, as in the above case, the income of a single individual is equivalent to the combined incomes of 3,000 heads of families. The trouble with us has been, and is, that we have arrogated to ourselves virtues that we possess not. We have proclaimed ourselves as being better than the rest of the world. We have assumed that the increased general comfort and higher wages of those who flocked to our shores, over and above what they had been accustomed to in the old world, was the measure of our patriotism and unselfish devotion to the cause of humanity, when in fact the amelioration of the poor emigrant was due to the operation of a simple though generally unknown law of political economy, viz: "Wages depend upon the margin of production, or upon the produce which labor can

obtain at the highest point of natural productive-
ness open to it without the payment of rent."

Land in America being comparatively easy of
access hitherto, the rate of wages in manufacturing centres or elsewhere has been determined by
what can be obtained by the laborer, working for
himself, upon land which he if free to enter upon
without the payment of rent. This law rests
upon that other law, more broad and general,
that men seek to gratify their desires with the
least exertion. The satisfied self-complacency
with which we view ourselves and our institutions
is not always shared by the distinguished writers
and publicists. John Stuart Mill reproached us
with being a nation of dollar hunters. Says
Canon Farrar: "American publicists have been
complaining of a wide prominence of dishonesty,
both in commerce and in politics; of defalcations,
of malfeasance, of sinister legislation, bought and
paid for by those whom it profits; of a rage for
amateur speculation, which was the ruin of the
peace, the fortune and the morals of many
homes."

"The year now drawing to a close," wrote an
American reviewer in 1884, "is of a nature calcu-

lated to humiliate and discourage those who have pride and faith in republican institutions. It is not necessary to name over the long and melancholy list. Political scandals and revelations of commercial dishonor are fresh in the minds of all, and all have observed the apparently lessening sense of the sacredness of marriage, the growing tendency towards stock gambling in all sections of the community, Much of the church's work depends upon her attitude towards wealth. Such expressions as the 'almighty dollar'; such proverbs as that quoted once by Wendell Phillips about springing after a dollar at any risk, even if it were put on the other side of hell; such a terrible sentence as that by Theodore Parker—'in the American church money is God'—point to a danger against prosperous nations, and England quite as much as America has ever to be on her guard.''

In brief the life work of Mr. Trevellick has been to appeal to those who hold the keys of the House of Have to be just and honorable and charitable in their dealings with the vast masses who hitherto have been the inhabitants of the House of Want. In so far as the appeal has been made to the moral, or, as we should now say, the altruistic sentiments of those who own all and who produce nothing; the cry for help in the name of a common brotherhood has met with no response, or responses of such rare and abortive character as to justify the remark of John Stuart Mill that when the desire is to permanently affect the material welfare of the people, small means not only produce small effects but they produce no effect at all.   Great and generous souls, such as Peter Cooper and Wendell Phillips in America, John Stuart Mill, Charles Kingsley, Thomas Hughes, Frederick Denison, Maurice and Frederick Harrison in England, Victor Hugo, Lamartine and Lamenais in France, Lassalle and Karl Marks in Germany, Lavaleye in Belgium, and Castelar in Spain, have stood forth as the apostles of a common humanity, believing in and trusting in a power that works for righteousness, diffused throughout the world for the healing of the nations and the uplifting of the human race; hidden and obscured, it is true, by the grasping, grinding, ignorant selfishness of men who become accretive maniacs in the race for wealth, but eventually to attain its full fruition in the reward of the just man made perfect. This is the necessary correlative of the law of Meliorism that reigns throughout the universe in accordance with the plan of a benign being, which not to accept is to land ourselves in the reign of a materialistic atheism, whose only escape from a melancholy and depressing pessimism is suicide.

But work, arduous and prolonged, was necessary if labor was to move towards emancipation. Agitation, education and organization were the lines upon which freedom was to be wrought out. The dreaming optimism of the disciples of Bastiat, with their gospel of contentment and non-resistance, based upon the theory that rent, monopoly, and stock gambling and millionaireism would die of apathy and inanition, found little favor in the political philosophy of Trevellick and his colleagues. With the largest trust · in a divine Providence, Trevellick always kept his powder dry. Believing that the Creator designed and willed the happiness of his creatures, and that truth and righteousness will ultimately prevail, he believed that the conditions had been given in irrevocable order, but that the combinations had been left in the hands of man, and that the character of the chain of human life varied as truth or falsehood, harmony or discord, seized the anvil upon which the links are forged.

Early imbued with the spirit of trades-unionism Trevellick began work upon the insular and exclusive lines which have always characterized bodies of craftsmen assembled together for the purpose of dealing with matters personal to themselves, local in character, and having in their views no signifance for the industrial world outside of their own peculiar craft.. Far be it from us to assert that trades unions have ever sanctioned the extreme suicidal doctrine that the man who receives three dollars per day has no part or parcel in the man receiving only a dollar a day. On the contrary they have a mission yet to fulfil, and have been of the greatest importance in the industrial upheaval of the past.

Speaking of the future of the astryan, factory and urban population, Prof. James E. Rogers, in his work, "Six Centuries of work and wages", says, "For this there is one remedy, extension of labor organization on the trade-union principle, but with considerable improvement in detail. If it be found that those callings only have prospered in which labor partnerships have devoloped and those Have prospered most in which the fundimental principles of such labor partnerships have been most prudently kept in mind and acted on, it stands to reason that an extention of the system to other callings, now notoriously underpaid, is the most obvious remedy for low wages and uncertain prospects. Such associations are a renewal of the best traits of the mediaeval guilds''.

The considerable improvement here spoken of has already been effected and embodied in the great and splendid organization which ramifies its nerves and arteries into every nook and corner of the United States and Canada, bidding fair to absorb unto itself every other agency and instrumentality designed for similar purposes. It is in the formation of this gigantic army that Trevellick's work and glory may be said to receive its consummation.

In the Knights of Labor he may be said to have organized victory.

Long before the Declarations of Principles formulated in the platform of the great order had been given to the public, Trevellick had stumped every state in the Union with a declaration identical in principle and method and differing but little in phraseology. Office and emoluments have, indeed, gone to others, but the pioneer in the wilderness preparing the way for the great edifice was Richard F. Trevellick.

The heartfelt sympathy and genuine sincerity no less than his natural gift of oratory have made him the most welcome visitant among wage workers of all those who, at present, espouse and champion the cause of labor. A confidence of many years standing has never been weakened by a single overt act. In a venal age he has escaped corruption; in the turmoil of party strife he has maintained a character above reproach. A frivolous sentiment never escaped his lips, for such was never engendered in his heart. The message he comes to deliver has been given forth with the earnestness and favor of a man who believes his own doctrine. He rivets the attention of his hearers by voicing the sentiments which well up in their own hearts, but which the unpracticed tongue is powerless to give expression.

A firm believer in manhood suffrage, he has

always urged upon his hearers, as one of the best
methods of education, the necessity of excercising
the mental faculties in political discrimination.
For this reason Trevellick has never failed to
scathingly denounce any attempts to defy the
lawfully constituted authorities by an exhibition
of mob rule. In so far as the evils under which
we labor, are the inseparable concomitants of
human life they must be born and endured with
the fortitude born of a Christian faith strong in
the hope of a resurrection to a more perfect state;
and in so far as they spring from a malid just-
ment of social forces, capable of a readjustment
at the hands of the legislator or statesmen, the
remedy is in our own hands, and should be sought
at the ballot box. Ignorance and incapacity in
weilding the right of franchise can never become
wisdom and discreation at the head of a mob. In
a speech delivered in Missouri not long before the
ill advised strike on the Southwestern roads he
said:

'Don't stand on the street corners and grum-
ble because things are not going on in the government to suit you, for the stream is always as pure
as the fountain from which it flows, and you are

the fountain.   Men walk about who do not know
the first principles of government, and who have
not the slightest real knowledge of the resources
of the country, its power, the condition of labor,
or any of the other questions that go to make up
the public intelligence.   *   *   *   Strikes are not
countenanced.   We want those differences between labor and capital settled by arbitration, as
stated above; not settled by hunger and blood-
shed, but by fair-minded reasoning on both sides.''

While never a believer in the Utopian dreams
of modern socialism, with its clear cut formulas,
and its great political alembic, into which society
is to be cast in the delusive hope of evolving an
aggregate altogether at variance with the units,
Trevellick has carefully steered clear, on the
other hand of the administrative Nihilism of which
we hear so much now a days. The peculiar phase
of this ''perfect liberty of the subject', theory,
fashionable in the United States, is known as the
laissez faire or let alone theory.   In this view of
the state its functions are minimized to a point
barely compatible with a mere nominal existence.
The peculiar significance of the labor question
arises from the fact of a wide diversity of opinion

prevalent among legislators and Knights of
Labor as to the wisdom or unwisdom of invoking
State and National aid in such matters as the
regulation of the hours of labor, the prohibition
of employment of children of tender years in factories and workshops; prescribing the conditions
upon which women and girls shall be employed;
the provision of proper fire and sanitary arrange-
ments; the inspection of mines and workshops;
the ownership of railroads and telegraphs; the establishment of post-office savings banks; State
aid to education, and compulsatory attendance;
the establishment of labor bureaus, and the na-
tionalization of land; the issuing and regulation
of the volume of currency. In the Knights of
Labor platform of principles, most of the foregoing subjects have been embodied as among
those requiring the aid and attention of legislatures, but while the vast majority of the members of the Knights of Labor are steadfast in the
belief of the soverign power of political machinery, several of the most thoughtful among the
leaders are uncompromising opponents of the
policy which looks to political action, even indi-
rectly, as a means for effecting anything bene-

ficial to the cause of labor. Most important, during the past two years, perhaps has been the question of a reduction of the hours of labor. Seeking at its inception the aid of the National legislature, a measure providing for its enforcement in the government establishments was passed through Congress, but remained inoperative upon the statute books for some years. Enthusiasm in State aid was thus dampened. The question remained in obeyance until the latter part of 1884, when it was again taken up and discussed with unwonted vigor and vehemence, and with an array of talent and argument worthy of the cause that invoked it. The great strikes along the line of industrial activity, during May, of this year, were the result of this agitation. It was sought to establish the eight-hour day by and through the labor organizations—no action soliciting the power of the state; but with few exceptions, the results obtained do not seem to afford much room for congratulation on the ground of superiority in choice of method.

While recognizing the soundness of the principle that a government should never be called upon to do those things which the people are

capable of doing for themselves. Trevellick has
always held that in certain directions, and under
proper limitations and restrictions, the aid of the
State is not only desirable but absolutely necessary. When the desire among any people is to
give immediate effect to wide spread sentiments
of reform, which in operation are beneficial in
character and wide reaching in influence, not only
are the agencies employed by the State certain
and direct above all others; but in general, have
no choice between consummating the work with its
aid and foregoing the attempt. Aside from any
theory, the opinion of Trevellick on the eighthour
question as being the product of a rich experience,
both in Australia and America, is extremely valuable. He does not express himself as being in
favor of a legislative enactment so stingent in its
provisions and rigorous in its enforcement as
to practically cut off the right of the individual
to determine for himself what number of hours
shall constitute a day's work, but he does believe
that every attempt on the part of legislators to
shorten the hours of labor by prohibitory enactments has been in the highest degree beneficial,
and therefore deserving of encouragement on the

part of workingmen. The government is, of
course, only but the voice of the corporate reason,
and functions and powers omnipotent no more
pertain to it, than to the individual whose mouth-
piece it is, and the statesmen or legislators bold
enough to inaugurate a policy at variance with
the time honored customs and prejudices of the
people will not have long to wait for a practical
demonstration of the erroneousness of the assumption. In spite of this, however, the fact
stands out clearly and indisputably, especially in
England, that the general, or average character
of legislation, as affecting the conditions of the
mining and the manufacturing operatives, has
been in the highest degree conducive to a higher
and better type of life. The recent experience of
American workingmen with the short-hour day
may serve to illustrate the manner in which the
law could be made effective as subserving the
deliberate collective opinion of the vast majority
of the citizens of the United States. The assumption is that the sentiment for a shorter
working day is everywhere participated in by
wage workers, that it could. be shown by statistics that manufacturers and middlemen could

well afford to pay the same compensation for
eight hours as is now paid for ten, the benefit
being a clear gain of two hours per day.   The
answer comes immediately from those who deprecate government interference that it be enough simply to point out the fact to the workingmen and
trust to the operation of the great and basic law of
political economy—that each seeks the greatest
gain with the least expenditure—to make the required beneficial change.   Any state meddling
will only defer or render migatory what may
otherwise be speedily and surely brought about.

But is this so?   "My experience," says Trevellick, "extending over thirty years in the countries of Europe, America and Australia, has been
a literal fullfilment of John Stuart Mill, which he
reached by a logical deduction from the facts of
human nature."   Given a conviction, is the adoption spontaneous?   "I answer," says Miil, "that
it would not be adopted unless the body of operatives bind themselves to one another to abide by
it.   A workingman who refused to work more
than eight or nine hours while there were others
who worked ten, would either not be employed at
all, or, if employed, must submit to lose a cor-

responding percentage of his wages. However
convinced he may be that it is to the interest of
the class to work short time, it is contrary to his
own interest to set the example, unless he is well
assured that all or most others will follow it.
But suppose a general agreement of the whole
class; might not this be effectual without the
sanction of law? Not unless enforced by opinion
with a rigor practically equal to law. For however beneficial the observance of the regulation
might be to the class collectively, the immediate
interest of every individual would lie in violating
it, and the more numerous those were who adhered to the rule, the more would individuals gain
by departing from it. If nearly all restricted
themselves, 'say to nine hours,' those who chose
to work ten would gain all the advantage of the
restriction, together with the profit of infringing
it; they would get ten hours' wages for nine
hours' work, and an hour's wages besides. I
grant that if a large majority adhered to the nine
hours there would be no harm done; the benefit
would be, in the main, secured to the class, while
those individuals who preferred to work harder
and earn more would have an opportunity of doing

so.   *   *   *   Probably, however, so many would
prefer the ten hours' work on the improved terms
that the limitations as a general practice; what
some did from choice others would soon be forced
to do from necessity, and those who had chosen
long hours for the sake of increased wages would
be forced in the end to work long hours for no
greater wages than before.''

Trevellick does not wish to be understood as
encouraging wageworkers to rely upon the State
to take the initiative in matters best left to their
own discretion; he desires rather to show how
the State may oftimes aid and abet a beneficial
project by giving it unity and precession at the
very outstart; lacking which, every social movement having for its object the overthrow of wrongs
deepseated in custom and venerable by antiquity
must be doomed, if not to ultimate failure. to a
growth so feeble and sporadic in character as
to practically confer no benefit upon its promo-
ters; or if conferring a benefit, to delay its coming
until old age and disinclination, by dulling the
senses, having chilled its enjoyment.

The arguments of those who deprecate all
State interference as a violation of the rights and

perogatives of individual sovereignty appear to
rest upon the assumption that all law and limi-
tation are in the nature of restraint. Coercion
and restraint are to be viewed as evils growing
out of the irrepressible desire of the tyrannical
and cunning portion of mankind to bind and en-
slave the remainder. All governments being by
their very nature founded in coercion and restraint, it follows that the less we have of them,
and the closer their claws are clipped, the better
for the cause of humanity. But as all governments derive their powers from the consent of
the governed, it is difficult to see how the abolition of government is possible; for the government manifestly is not something outside of and
objective to the community which gives it birth,
ruling it as an external sovereign; but is simply
the form of activity of the units, which compose
or make up the aggregate known as the public.
Individuals only are the truly exitsent. The
law of human natue is association. The law of
human progress is association in equality. As
necessarily corelatable and conditioning these,
we have that other law—the inalienable right of
every individual to the pursuit of liberty, limited

only by the like right of every other individual. Hence arise the mutual concessions and limitations incidental thereto, and inseparable from, the well ordered life of men dwelling together in a state of society—that is government. A man can no more transcend the facts given in the common experience of the race than wing his flight through interplanetery space. Thinking will not add a cubit to his stature, nor prayer, nor supplication increase the number of his senses.

Anarchy, or the liberty of the individual, can mean nothing but a reversion to Hobbe's state of nature, or right of war, that is, barbarism. The ideal of the anarchist, in so far as it is an improvement on the present order of things, is the very child of that Law and Morality which he so effects to despise. Society and the state are the indispensable conditions to liberty and the real freedom of the individual; outside of these is the untamed impulse of a savage animality, redhanded in bloody, inhuman deeds, and giving full vent to every wild impulse sweeping athwart the soul. The very restraints imposed by mutual limitations in a state of association are the means whereby the soul becomes conscious of its freedom

and exaltation above the realm of the mere sen-
suous. Freedom is possible only where government is; and government is possible only where
the reason has become a law unto itself by mark-
ing out the metes and bounds beyond which it is
resolved not to pass. If it be said·that the foregoing is a mere begging of the question; and that
if all coercive government were a way, a condition
of society far preferable to that which now exists
would be the result, we reply that the assertion
is contradicted by the facts of universal history,
as well as by the laws determining the growth of
the social organism. The bond of its association,
as formulated in the decrees of a governing power, once loosened or destroyed, every nation has
had but one tale to unfold—first, decay; then dis-
integration; then, final extinction.

The genesis from a barbaric progress from
tribal anarchy into the first stages of civilization,
we are not here called upon to explain; suffice it
to say, that the facts are given in experience, and,
whether capable or not of being reduced to any
known laws of evolutionary development, subsequent progress has always been in class depend-
ence upon ability to hold and control the members

of the community within the rigidly formulated decrees of a centralized authority—government.

The question of government or no government, then, resolves itself into a question of method. Farther than this it cannot go. That all governments in the past have been very bad we do not deny; that those now in existence, without exception, have miserably failed to secure the maximum of human happiness, no enlightened person will gainsay; but the question of their abolition, even if desirable, is not debatable. The problem of Knights of Labor and other kindred organizations is to direct the flow, not to dam the course. All discussion beyond these limits may serve as an intellectual gymnastic, but for all practical purposes is stale and unprofitable.

We have adverted to the question of the limits of state sovereignty at some length because of the earnestness with which some of the leading members of the Knights of Labor, as well as certain economists, are urging workingmen to eschew all political action and to remain passive while the machinery of government passes into the hands of those who have hitherto wielded its powers so potently in the accomplishment of selfish aims.

Time and time again have the workingmen been beguiled with the cry, "We must have a man at the head of the government affairs who will conduct it on business principles." Of all mountebanks at the head of affairs. your business man is surely the greatest. Generally a millionaire and in the nature of affairs out of sympathy with the class which makes millionaireism possible, he is usually a man of unbounded reputation and very little character. He runs amuck of every political problem, on the assumption that not the law, but "chaos and eternal night," reign in social affairs. When it is proposed to try the efficiency of the law in ameliorating the condition of the masses by nationalizing the land, shortening the hours of labor, prohibiting the employment of child labor, etc., he exercises the demon of reform by his trusty talismans—doctrine and demagogue—following which he deems the cause of good government on the high road to perpetuity.

What are business principles in politics? Buckle knew: "It was Adam Smith who, far more than any other man, introduced the conception of uniform and necessary sequence into the

apparently capricious phenomena of wealth, and
who studied those phenomena by the aid of principles, of which selfishness alone supplied the
data.   According to his views, the employers of
labor have, as employers, no benevolence, no sympathy, no virtue of any kind; their sole aim is
their own selfish interest.   They are constantly
engaged in a tacit, if not in an open, combination
to prevent the lower ranks from being benefitted
by a rise in wages; and they sometimes combine
for the purpose even of depressing those wages
below their actual rate.   Having no bowels of
compassion, they think only of themselves.   The
idea of their wishing to mitigate the inequalities
of fortune is to be exploded as one of the chimeras
of that protective spirit, which imagined that society could not go on unless the richer classes
helped the poor ones, or 'sympathized with their
troubles.'   In years of scarcity 'they make better
terms for themselves; they lower wages just at
the moment when sympathy for misfortune would
have raised them; and as they find that their employes, besides being more remunerative, are, by
poverty, made more submissive, they consider
that scarcity is a blessing and that dear years
are more favorable to industry than cheap ones.''

It was Mr. Business Principle who was so swift-footed in pointing out to working men the treasonable act of the Michigan legislature when it sought to invade their right of individual sovereignty by the passage of the ten hour act. It was Mr. B. P. who induced them to waive their privilege under the statute, by signing an iron-clad contract, while at the same time he denied their right to band together in labor organizations for mutual protection.

Suppose wage workers would be a little more active in affairs political and make it possible to tender to Mr. Business Principle the advice Palmerston once gave to a meddling minister, "suppose you try learning it alone." Would it not be rational to think it possible that some means might be devised by which a larger share of the wealth they create might accrue to themselves? "The strike and the boycott are, after all," says Trevellick, "but indifferent weapons with which to storm a camp so strongly entrenched as that of Monopoly." Paper bullets have a more subtle and insinuating manner than the leaden ones. And what is more, the ammunition is mostly on our side. Strong in

the consciousness of the justness of our cause,
and with men of the stamp of integrity to direct,
and such men as Henry George, and Schilling and
Leavitt to write and reason, may we not hope
that ere the present generation shall pass away,
full and fair acknowledgement of the efforts of
the great order of the Knights of Labor to up-
lift and enlighten shall be made to the nations of
the world?

These in brief are some salient features of
Trevellick's thought and busy life, and which we
are sure will be welcome to his many admirer's,
and also to those who love to hear the short and
simple annals of the poor.   The world indeed has
been his country; his religious creed to do good.
He had been trained in the best' of schools—the
school of experience-for here only can the wise,
equally with the fool, learn wisdom.   The globe
aptly symbolized the field of his operation, for he
has proclaimed to European, Asiatic, African and
Indian alike the doctrines of universal brotherhood, and grew eloquent in denunciation of the
accursed doctrine that "the blackman had no
right to respect." He supplemented his vast experience of men and things by keeping abreast of

political economy, his associates being quite as much the learned as the unlearned. Toiling and plodding on, sometimes weary but never discouraged, he has held his course onward towards the beacon light, assured that help was not far off. He has lived to see the manumission of the black slave, but the struggle impending in Europe and America in the manumission of the white and black slaves from the bondage of concentrated Capital he has not lived to see. Rent interest and profits have sown dragon's teeth. What shall the harvest be? Armed men or slaves?

CHAPTER VIII.

IN conclusion, the editor of the Galveston News wishes to offer a few words on the question, "Are we tending to revolution?"

"The storm-portending clouds that rear their darkening heads along the horizen of the Western World, rest now in seeming solumn stillness, save where, afar off the lightening's flash and deep-voiced thunder, in dull reverberation give warning of the hidden tumult, but the blinding fury of the whirlwind cannot long be delayed. The causes efficient to provoke the downpour are present in America no less than in England, Ireland, Belgium, France, Germany, Russia and Spain; and ere the present century shall pass away, changes fraught with blessings to mankind or charged with the night of anarchy and chaos, will be upon us. It is said that the last decade of the past several centuries has been devoted to revolt, if so it may be possible to formulate a rythmic law of revolution and nothing, perhaps, can save the nations of the old world from a bloody birth, as the necessary precursor of regeneration and emancipation; but unto America, still in the glory and strength of young and vigorous manhood, it is given to escape the deepflung roar and wreck of the approaching deluge if she but heed betimes the austere councils and imitate the actions of the great men who reared upon Puritanic base, the fabric of the great Republic.

"In the days of '76 America bred patriots and orators; to-day, millionaire demagogues and rhetoricans. Then an American had no time for the base pursuit of money making; the battle of life was before him and his country expected every man to do his duty. To-day the measure of man is gold, and his worth is told in terms of the dollar. Formerly, Americans found the men whom they delighted where the Romans found Cincinnatus—at the plow; now, all kneel in obeisance to the high priest of the Golden Calf, whose popularity is as the number of victims immolated upon his altar. Fifty years ago men were divided by distance and to-day by caste. Progress is conditioned on equality in association.

There is no other way.   Backward or forward we must go.

"Being is known only by activity, for absolute rest is inconceivable.   Things move rapidly in America, but the movement is of a dual character.   In the manipulation of force and matter for the service of man our progress has been unrivaled by any people, ancient or modern, while in the domain of ethics, or morals, or retrocession is as humiliating as it is palpable and apparent. We have gained great riches but have placed them in few hands.   That the few may revel in luxury and splendor, the many are thrust into blighting poverty.   To the few we have given power over man's sustenance, and with it power over men's wills.   We have, indeed, moved onward, but not upward.   We have advanced to other points on the same plane, but not to higher levels.

"To perform our duty or not to perform it, is the question; and upon the answer depends the position we are to occupy among the nations of the earth.   Such as is the character of the units, such also will be the character of the national morality.   For the past quarter of a century our

course has been towards the City of Destruction.
If we can but appreciate the immortal maxim of
Kant: Duty? Wondrous thought, that workest
neither by fond insinuation, flattery, nor by any
threat, but merely by holding up thy naked law
in the soul, and so extorting for thyself always
reverence, if not obedience, before whom all appe-
tites are dumb, however secretly they rebel;
whence thy origin?' or if we follow the teachings
of that superb American, Wendell Phillips, all
may yet be well.

"If, on the other hand, we continue in the policy and traditions of the past thirty years, guag-
ing human souls and bodies by an odious law of
supply and demand, dealing in the heart and brain
of man as in a commodity, quoting human blood
and muscle in terms of merchandise—millionaires
on one hand, paupers on the other—millions upon
millions toiling and plodding in grinding, bitter
poverty, that a few men and women may become
a veritable parasite class in the community, pa-
rading in insolent ostentation the wealth of which
others have been exploited, and which needs on
the part of the exploiter but to be born with the
despicable faculties of cunning and rapacity pre-

turnaturally developed, then this is the story
briefly told:

"This is the moral of all human tales.
'Tis but the same rehearsal of the past:
First freedom, and then glory; when that
　　　fails,
Wealth, vice, corruption, barbarism at last;
And history with all her volumes vast
　　　Hath but one tale."

Shall nature abdicate?　Will law forego her
ancient reign that America may escape?　Is not
the God of the Egyptian, the Hebrew, the Greek,
and the Roman, also the God of the American?

CHAPTER IX.

THE subjoined treatise on money was compiled and written by Mr. Trevellick shortly before his death, and styled:

MONEY AND PANICS.

"Panics, with all the evils that follow in their train, must continue to curse the American people until there is a righteous solution of the financial question.—R. T.

"This pamphlet has been prepared for the careful consideration of the thinking public. Owing to the unsettled condition of monetary affairs, the losses sustained to this nation during the last six months have been enormous. Millions of laborers have been unemployed, and this lack of employment has brought in its train miseries untold. This misery has largely resulted from lack of money to do business with. Three years ago the national banks began the contraction of the currency, reducing from 1890 to the end of the year 1892 their out-standing circulation from three hundred million dollars to one hundred and twenty-seven million dollars. Then followed the stopping of the coinage in silver. This was another contraction of fifty million dollars. Then followed the order of the Secretary of the Treasury, redeeming silver certificates in gold, which resulted in another contraction of one hundred and fifty million dollars, making in three years a contraction of three hundred and seventy-three millions. To this must be added very many millions more that have been lost, burned or otherwise destroyed, but which has always been counted as part of the circulation by the Treasury Department, but is not there.

"The contraction took the life blood out of the nation, and idleness followed as a natural consequence. This contraction of the currency forced idleness of factories, idleness of trade, idleness of transportation and idleness of six millions of persons. So this increase of idleness has increased drunkenness, increased poverty, increased murder, increased robbery, increased suicide, increased assassination, and increased crime of every description, and it all begins with the contraction of the currency and idleness of money, which compels the idleness of every other class of honest industry.

"If these miseries have come upon the people by reason of mal-administration of monetary affairs, is it not prudent to ask the question, 'What is money and how shall it be regulated?' Money is a medium of exchange created by law, by which the value of all commodities produced are represented and exchanged, but it is not money as soon as it passed out of the jurisdiction of the government which created it.

"Whence do governments derive the power to create money and set a legal value upon it? Coining or issuing money is an act of sovereignty and belongs to the people.

"Nations under despotic governments have had this right usurped by their rulers. The money of those nations is issued by the fiat of the despot and by arbitrary power. In representative governments this power is delegated to their representatives, either through legal enactments acquiesced in by the people, or specifically stated in the constitution.

" The constitution of the United States is very explicit on this point. It says: (Art. 1 Sec. 8.) 'Congress shall have power to coin money and regulate the value thereof, and of foreign coins, and fix the standard of weights and measures.' In adopting the constitution the people surrendered this right of sovereignty to their representatives in the two houses of congress, so that whatever power the people possessed before the adoption of the Constitution, Congress has possessed it since its adoption.

" The Constitution does not prohibit Congress from making anything but gold and silver a legal tender in the payment of debt.

"In defining the power of a state (Art. 1 Sec. 10) it says: 'No state shall enter into any treaty, alliance or confederation, grant letters of marque and reprisal, coin money, emit bills of credit, make anything but gold and silver coin a tender in the payment of debts, pass any bill of attainder, ex post facto law, or law impairing the obligation of contracts, or grant any title of nobility.' This provision applies to the power of individual states and has nothing to do with the power of Congress.

"We learn by consulting "Sumner's Reminisences of Colonial Times," that the Massachusetts colony was the first to issue money.   This occurred in 1690, six years before the Bank of England was established.   It was neither gold nor silver.   It was paper money, issued in bills of from five shillings to five pounds, and the issue amounted to seven thousand pounds sterling. The notes were made receivable for all dues to the Colonial Government, and circulated at par with gold for twenty years. In 1703 an additional fifteen thousand pounds was issued, and made legal tender for both public and private debts. One hundred an l fifty thousand pounds were issu d in 1716, and were loaned to the people of the Colony at five per cent. per annum in specific sums on real estate security for a term of years. Fifty thousand pounds more were issued in 1720, making in all two hundred and twenty-two thousand pounds, or one million one hundred and ten thousand dollars.   The issue of this money enabled the colony to declare itself clear of debt in 1773.

"Rhode Island issued bills in 1720 which were legal tender for all debts.   Connecticut is-

sued money from 1709 to 1731.   New York issued
money first in 1709, Pennsylvania in 1723, Maryland in 1733, Delaware in 1739, Virginia in 1753,
and South Carolina in 1703.   The first issue of
Virginia bore five per cent. interest and was soon
locked up by hoarders as a safe investment.

"Thomas Jefferson says: 'The next issue
was bottomed on a redeeming tax and bore no
interest.'   Those bills, he says, 'were readily
received and never depreciated a farthing.'   He
further says that several hundred thousand dollars of this Colonial paper money remained in
circulation more than twenty years at par with
gold with no other basis of advantage than being
receivable for debts and taxes.

"At this time the Colonies were under the
control of the English Government, with governors appointed by the Crown.   Their legislatures
were elected by the people.   The Government
had passed no law providing for issuing money by
the Colonies, so they asserted their right of
sovereignty and provided the necessary legislation for themselves.

"So long as there was no law of the English
government prohibiting this exercise of sover-

eignty, the bills issued by the Colonies were, to all intents and purposes, the money of the people, and circulated as such, at par with coin. In 1751, forty-eight years after the first bills were issued, when the growing prosperity of the Colonies aroused the jealousy of the money lords, they prevailed on Parliament to pass a law forbidding the issue of any more money by the Colonies. Not satisfied with that, in 1763 they procured the passage of a law declaring all acts passed by the Colonies providing for the issue of money void.

"Here is another instance in which the fact is demonstrated that money is created by law. The law of the Colonies made these bills issued by them money, and they performed all the functions of money. The English government, being superior to the Colonial governments, declared it was not money by declaring the legislation of the Colonies providing for the issue void, when it ceased to be money at all.

"The success attending the use of this money in developing the weak, struggling and neglected Colonies into wealthy and prosperous communities was educating the people to understand that they could be independent of the usurers of the world, and hence must be crushed out in order to satisfy the greed of the money power, who dictated the policy of the British Government, just as the same class now dictate the policy of the American Government.

"Judge Warwick Martin, on the fiat money of England on page 143 says: 'Before the invention by England of bank notes by which one dollar of coin was made to represent twenty dollars of his liabilities, and before the people were enslaved by the issue of interest bearing bonds, governments supported their wars and provided for their newly contracted debts by increasing the fiat or legal tender value of their coins or by adding greatly to the copper alloy therein. By these means they added greatly to the amount of coin in circulation.'

"This was done by a long line of English Kings, among whom were Edward III., Henry IV., Henry VII., Henry VIII. and Queen Elizabeth. Each one of these monarchs reduced the quantity of pure metal by making it light weight or by substituting copper for pure metal, sufficient to increase the quantity of money to meet the demand. These fiats of monarchs did not re-

late to paper money.   Until 1694 no paper money
existed.   Their fiats related to and changed
the   metallic   money,   which   was   then   the   only
money in use.   These fiats always changed the
fiats of their predecessors upon the same thrones,
the fineness of the coins having been established
by the fiats of the former Kings.

"When Elizabeth changed the fineness of the
coins of her realm, increasing the alloy therein, a
citizen refused to receive the new coin in payment
of a debt contracted before the coin was made.
A suit at law was commenced to collect the debt
in old coin.   The defendent pleaded a tender of
the coin of the Queen to the full amount of the
claim.   The most learned Judges were called upon to hear and try the case.   The decission of the
court was in favor of the defendent.   It sanctioned the money of the Queen and the right of
the sovereign to issue money as she saw proper.
The report of the case is very voluminous and in
substance is as follows:

"What six things or circumstances ought to
concur to make money lawful: first, weight; second, fineness; third, impression; fourth, denomi-
naton; fifth, authority; sixth, proclamation.   For

every piece of money ought to have a certain proportion of weight or poise, and a certain proportion of purity or fineness, which is called alloy;
and also every piece ought to have a certain form
or impression which may be knowable and dis-
tinguishable, for as wax is not the seal without
the stamp, so metal is not money without an impression, and money is named from 'Monendo'
(informing,) because by its impression it informs
whose money it is. 'Whose image is this?''
asked Christ. 'Ceaser's.' 'Then render unto
Ceaser the things that are Ceaser's.' Also every
peice of money ought to have a denomination or
valuation, for how much shall it be accepted or
paid, as for a penny, a groat, or a shilling, and
all this ought to be by the authority or command-
ment of the Prince, for otherwise money is not
lawful, and it ought to be published by proclamation, for otherwise the money is not current.

"Thus for hundreds of years the kings of
England changed either the fineness of the coin
or the weight thereof, and were sustained in doing
so by the common law and the decisions of their
highest courts. The fiats of the kings created
and regulated all money of the country. In the

reign of Elizabeth the sterling money was created by her fiat. It was all silver. A troy pound of silver was coined into twenty shillings, which were a pound sterling. The silver was made 925 parts pure in the 1,000 parts, and 75 parts alloy. This fiat stood as the English standard of fineness of silver from that time till now. But by a subsequent fiat of Parliament, though this fineness was continued, a troy pound of silver was coined into sixty-two shillings, making more than three times as much money out of the pound of silver than had been made by the former fiat. The pound of silver by this fiat was made to have more than three times the money value it had under the fiat of the Queen.

"During the Reign of Queen Catherine, of Russia, that Government was at war with Turkey. The metallic money was not sufficient to sustain the nation. The Government issued treasury notes, which carried it through the war successfully. It did the same thing in order to carry on its war with Napoleon. So popular was this national fiat money with the people that before it was withdrawn from circulation it commanded a premium over coin.

"By the fiat of the British Government the notes of the Bank of England were made legal tender from 1797 till 1823. This money sustained the Government through its wars with the French, and the war of 1812 with the United States. In 1813 the allied powers of Russia, Prussia and England, in their attempt to conquer Napoleon, discovered that their gold and silver money had retired from circulation and could not be relied upon. The notes of the banks of the several powers were not international money and would not support them. The three nations, by agreement, issued a joint paper fiat money, with which they prosecuted the war to a successful termination.

"The credit of France was shaken after the abdication of Louis Phillipe and the change to a republican form of government in 1848. The bank of France was unable to procure coin to conduct its legitimate business; its circulation was necessarily greatly reduced, which threw the people into idleness for want of means to stimulate the industries of the country. In this condition of things the Government took charge of the bank and by its fiat made the notes full legal tender and increased its issues two hundred millions. These notes depended entirely on the credit of the Government for their par value, for the bank had suspended specie payment, and has never professed to pay coin since.   These notes are preferred to coin by the people on account of their convenience and the implicit confidence they place greater in the integrity of the Government.

"In 1770 the Russian Government issued its own notes, which sustained the Government through two wars, and the people were so well satisfied with them as money that they commanded a premium over coin.

"The English Government made the notes of the Bank of England full legal tender money from 1797 to 1823, and we are informed by history that the nation never enjoyed so much prosperity as it did during that twenty-six years.   In that period her currency was inflated from forty to one hundred and twenty-seven millions.

"The Government of the United States issued treasury notes in 1812, 1813, 1814 and 1815, and made them legal tender for all debts due the Government.   The people were so well satisfied with this money that it required two acts of Congress to withdraw it from circulation.

"Treasury notes were issued and made lawful money of the United States in 1837 and used until 1848, at the close of the Mexican war, being always at par with coin and were at a premium in Mexico during the war.   During the great panic of 1857, when the banks suspended, the Government issued twenty millions of legal tender notes, with which the business of the country was transacted.

"Since 1861 the Congress of the United States has exercised its legitimate power in the issue of demand notes, legal tenders, 7-30 notes, three years interest notes, compound interest notes, certificates of indebtedness, certificates of deposits for coin, and three per cent. interest certificates. These were all made money of the Government and circulated as such.

"Benjamin Franklin, when called before a committee of Parliament in 1764, summed up in these words: 'On the whole, no method has hitherto been formed to establish a medium in trade, in lieu of coin, equal in all its advantages to bills of credit, founded on sufficient taxes for discharging it at the end of the time, and in the meantime made a general legal tender.'

"Thomas Jefferson, who has the reputation of having drafted the Constitution, and should certainly understand with what power it clothes Congress, when writing to Mr. Epps on the danger of bank associations, says: 'Bank paper must be suppressed and the circulating medium must be restored to the nation, to whom it rightly belongs.   *   *   *   It is the only resource which can never fail them, and it is an abundant one for every necessary purpose.   Treasury bills, bottomed on taxes, bearing or not bearing interest as may be found necessary, thrown into circulation, will take the place of so much gold and silver.'

"Albert Gallatin, who was twelve years secretary of the treasury, said, 'The right of issuing paper money as currency, like that of gold and silver, belongs exclusively to the Nation.'

"Daniel Webster, in a speech delivered in the United States Senate on the 31st of January, 1833, said: 'The Constitutional power vested in Congress over the legal currency of the country is one of the very highest powers, and the exercise of this power is one of the strongest bonds of

the union of the states.   It is not to be doubted
that the Constitution intended that Congress
should exercise a regulating power—a power both
necessary and salutary—over that which should
constitute the actual money of the country,
whether that money were coin or the representative of coin.'

"President Madison said in his message to
Congress in 1816: 'It is essential that the nation
should possess a currency of equal value, credit
and use wherever it may circulate.   The Constitution has intrusted Congress, exclusively, with
the power of creating and regulating a currency
of that description.'

"In a speech delivered in the Senate on September 23rd, 1837, Mr. Calhoun used this language: 'The Constitution does not stop with this
grant of the coinage power to Congress.   It expressly prohibits the states from emitting bills of
credit.   The states are, therefore, prohibited
from issuing paper for circulation on their own
credit, and this provision furnishes additional and
strong proof that all circulation, whether coin or
paper, was intended to be subject to the regulation and control of Congress.   The Constitution

declares that Congress shall have power to regulate commerce, not only with foreign nations but among the states.   This is a full and complete grant, and must include authority over everything which is a part of commerce or essential to commerce.   And is not money essential to commerce?'

"Mr. Dallas, who was Secretary of the Treasury in 1816, said in his report of that year: 'Whenever the emergency occurs that demands a change of system it seems necessarily to follow that the authority which was alone competent to establish the national coin is alone competent to create a national substitute.'

"John C. Calhoun said in a speech in the United States Senate, on the 18th of December, 1837: 'I would ask, then, why should the government mingle its credit with that of private corporations?   No one can doubt that the government credit is better than that of any bank—more stable and more safe.   *   *   *   Why, let me ask, should the government be exposed to such difficulties as the present, by mingling its credit with that of the banks, when it could be exempt from all such by using by itself its own safer credit?'

"President Jackson said in his message to

Congress in 1829: 'I submit to the wisdom of the legislature whether a national one (currency,) founded on the credit of the government and its resources, might not be devised, which would obviate all Constitutional difficulties and at the same time secure all the advantages of the government and the country that were expected to result from the present bank.'

"The Hon. John M. Bright, in a speech before the House of Representatives in 1880, said: 'I shall not elaborate the constitutionality of this subject, but will give a synopsis which I submit to the consideration of any of the objectors in relation to it.   I say it has been held to be constitutional by Congress is various acts and by the courts in repeated cases; that it has been held to be constitutional by both parties; that it has been held to be constitutional by a majority of the state courts of the United States; that it has been repeatedly held constitutional by the Supreme Court of the United States, and it has been acquiesced in by the people of the United States and they have adopted it as their money of account, and that the man who would rush against this question with such an array of authority against him must be struck with an unaccountable presumption.   *   *   *   Up to the time of the decision of the Supreme Court of the United States in the case of Knox against Lee (12 Wallace 457) there were fifteen state courts which had affirmed the constitutionality of it, independent of the Supreme Court of the United States.   I have six cases from the Supreme Court of the United States: Knox vs. Lee (12 Wallace 457), Trebilcox vs. Wilson (12 Wallace 687), Dooley vs. Smith (13 Wallace 604), Bigler vs. Walker (14 Wallace 297); R. R. Co. vs. Johnson (15 Wallace 195), Broderick vs. McGram (15 Wallace 639); all affirming the constitutionality of it.   Chief Justice Chase himself, in Hepburn vs. Griswold, stated that the constitutionality had never been called in question except as to its retrospective effect, and then by the submission of the people to this and the contemporaneous construction of other courts bring to its relief a general principle of law which has all the force of law itself.   The mere fact that this is a concurrence is an argument in favor of the proposition which is concurred in by the different courts.'

"Here is an array of testimony which it would

seem ought to satisfy the mind of every honest
doubter that the Constitution clothes Congress
with unlimited power in the selection of the material of which it creates the money of the United
States. I will give a synopsis of the decisions
rendered by the Supreme Court of the United
States in the cases of Knox vs Lee and Parker vs.
Davis, which were consolidated and brought before the court and fully argued for the purpose of
obtaining a decision from that body which would
put the question of the constitutionality of the
legal tender acts of Congress and its power to
determine when such power should be exercised
fully set at rest. I give the language of the court
as recorded in 12 Wallace, United States Supreme
Court reports. It says:

" 'Before we can hold the legal tender acts
unconstitutional we must be convinced that they
were not appropriate means or means conducive to
the execution of any or all the powers of Congress
or the Government, not appropriate in any degree (for we are not the judges of that degree of
appropriateness) or we must hold that they were
prohibited.'

"On page 542 of these reports we find the
following language:

" 'The degree of the necessity for any Congressional enactment, or the relative degree of its appropriateness is for consideration in Congress, and not here. When the law is not prohibited, and is really calculated to effect any of the objects of the government, to undertake here to enquire into the degree of the necessity, would be to pass the line which circumscribes the Judicial department and tread on Legislative grounds.'

"It will be seen by the above quotations that the Court did not decide the simple question of the Constitutional power of Congress to issue legal tenders in time of war, but the whole matter of the necessity of all acts for whatever purpose not prohibited by the Constitution. The Court continues on page 545.'

" 'The Constitution was intended to frame a government as distinguished from a league or compact—a government supreme in some things over state and people. It was designed to provide the same currency having a uniform legal value in all the states. It was for this reason the power to coin money and regulate its value was conferred on the Federal goverment, while the same power to emit bills of credit was with-

held from the states. The states can no longer
declare what shall be money or regulate its value.
Whatever power there is over the currency is
vested in Congress. If the power to declare
what is money is not vested in Congress it is
annihilated.'

"Still further on page 546, the Court says:
'And generally when one of such powers was
expressly denied to the states only, it was for the
purpose of rendering the Federal power more
complete and exclusive. How sensible then, its
framers must have been that emergencies might
arise where the precious metals might prove in-
adequate to the necessities of the Government
and the demands of the people, when it is remembered that paper money was almost exclusively
in use in the States as a medium of exchange,
and when the great evil sought to be remedied
was the want of uniformity in the current value
of money. It might be argued, we say, that the
gift of power to coin money and regulate the
value thereof was understood as conveying general power over the currency and which had belonged to the States, and which they had surrendered.'

"By this decision the whole power over the currency, whether metallic or paper, is vested in Congress, by the Constitution, to regulate in its wisdom for the interests of the whole people. This question being settled, the court proceeds to decide upon the Government issues as money legal tender. On pages 548 and 549 in says:

"'By the obligation of a contract to pay money is to pay that which the law shall recognize as money when the payment is to be made. If there is anything settled by decision it is this, and we do not understand it to be controverted? No one ever doubted that a debt of one thousand dollars contracted before 1834 could be paid with one hundred eagles coined after that year, though they contained no more gold than ninety-four eagles when the contract was made; and is not because of the intrinsic value of the coin, but its legal value. The eagles coined after 1834 were not money before they were authorized by law, and had they been coined before, without a law fixing their legal value, they could no more have paid a debt than uncoined buillion or cotton or wheat.'

"Once more, on page 553: 'It is hardly cor-

rect to speak of a standard of value.   The Constitution does not speak of it.   It contemplates a
standard for that which has gravity or extention,
but value is an ideal thing.   The coinage acts fix
its unit as a dollar, but the gold or silver thing
we call a dollar is in no sense a representation of
it.   There might never have been a piece of the
denomination of a dollar.   *   *   *   It will be
seen that we hold the acts of Congress constitutional as applied to contracts made before or after
their passage.'

"Attorney General Ackerman, in this case,
arguing in favor of the constitutionality, said:
Congress has never hesitated to enact what
should be a legal tender in payment of debts.
The right thus to enact has been assumed in
twenty-four statutes, passed in the presidencies
of Washington, Jefferson, Madison, Munroe,
Jackson, Tyler, Polk, Fillmore, Pierce, Lincoln
and Johnson.   *   *   *   The Constitution no-
where declares that nothing shall be money unless
made of metal.'

"In the case of Bigler vs. Walker (14 Wallace p. 297) a decree ordering the payment in coin
of a debt contracted before the passage of the

Legal Tender Acts reversed on the authority of the Legal Tender Cases (12 Wallace Knox vs. Lee and Parker vs. Davis).

"Juilliard vs. Greenman (U. S. Reports vol. 110 p. 41): 'Congress has the constitutional power to make the treasury notes of the United States a legal tender in payment of private debts in time of peace as well as in time of war.'

"Under the act of May 31st, 1878, Ch 146, which enacts that when any United States legal tender notes may be redeemed or received into the treasury, and shall belong to the United States, they shall be reissued and paid out again, and kept in circulation.   Notes so reissued are a legal tender.

"Submitted to Supreme Court, January, 1884, decided March, 1884, the opinion of the Court being delivered by Justice Gray.

'Upon full consideration of the case, Court is unanimously of the opinion that it cannot be distinguished in principle from the cases heretofore determined, reported under the names of the Legal Tender cases (12 Wallace,) Dooley vs. Smith (13 Wallace,) R. R. Co. vs. Johnson (15

Wallace,) and Maryland vs. R. R. Co. (22 Wallace.')

"Cooley, in his "Constitutional limitations" chapter 2, page 13 quotes as follows from the Constitution:

" 'Congress has power to make all laws which shall be necessary and proper for carrying into execution the foregoing powers, and all other powers vested by the Constitution in the government of the United States or in any department or officer thereof.'

"A note on this passage (exparte Curtis, 106 U. S., 471) reads as follows: 'Within the legitimate scope of this grant Congress can determine for itself what is necessary.'

"Justice Gray is also quoted as follows (Legal Tender cases, 110 U. S., 421)

" 'Congress, as the Legislature of a sovereign nation, being expressly empowered by the Constitution to lay and collect taxes to pay the debts and provide for the common defense and general welfare of the United States, and to borrow on the credit of the United States, and to coin money and regulate the value thereof and of foreign coin, and being clearly authorized, as incidental to the exercise of those great powers, to emit bills of credit, to charter National Banks, and to provide a National currency for the whole people, in the form of coin, treasury notes and National Bank bills; and the power to make the notes of the government a legal tender in the payment of private debts being one of the powers belonging to sovereignty in other civilized nations, and not expressly held from Congress by the Constitution, we are irresistibly impelled to the conclusion that the impressing upon the treasury notes of the United States, the quality of being a legal tender in the payment of private debts is an appropriate means conducive and plainly adapted to the undoubted powers of Congress, and therefore, within the meaning of that instrument, necessary and proper for carrying into execution the powers vested by this Constitution in the government of the United States.'

"In the leading Michigan case on this subject, that of Van Husan vs. Kanouse (13 Michigan p. 303), the point at issue was, 'Whether the law making the treasury notes in question a legal tender in payment of debts is within the constitutional power of Congress.' The decision delivered by

Judge Campbell is, in effect, as follows: 'This question having been answered in the affirmative by most of these courts who have been required to decide it, (including the Court of Appeals of New York), we should not deem it necessary to reconsider it were it not a question of public importance.   *   *   *   Reasons for doubting the validity of the law—denial of power in Congress to authorize the emission of any bills of credit at all, and the denial of the right to make anything but gold and silver a legal tender. The power to issue bills of credit has not been expressly given, and it is claimed such power should be expressed. Power was designedly denied by the convention which framed the Constitution.   *   *   *   Question of express power certainly not found in the Constitution.   *   *   *   In the absence of any prohibition is power fairly deducible from those provisions which declare the duties and authority designed to be vested in the General Government?   *   *   *   We are satisfied that the United States is not prohibited from issuing bills of credit (p 333).   In the denial of the right of Congress to make anything legal tender except gold or silver, it has been contended that there is no express

power in Congress to declare anything a legal
tender.   *   *   *   No states shall coin money,
emit bills of credit or make anything but gold or
silver a legal tender in the payment of debt, is
not an enabling clause.   If there is anything expressed in the Constitution upon the subject of
legal tender it is the clause that Congress shall
have power to coin money and regulate the value
thereof and of foreign coins.   The Constitution
clearly designed to take all questions of currency,
whether paper or metal, from the hands of several
states, and we think it is in the discretion of Congress to make of its tokens, whether of one substance or another, tenders in such amounts or for
such purposes as may be determined upon.'

"The state cases in which the question of the
constitutionality has been passed upon may be
found in the following reports:

"Carpenter vs. Northfield Bank (39 Vt., 46).
"Shollenberger vs. Brinton (52 Pa., st. 9).
"Verges vs. Gibony (33 Mo., 458).
"Brown vs. Welch (26 Ind., 116).
":Latham vs. U. S. (1 Ct. of C. L., 149).
"Lick vs. Faulkner (25 Cal., 404).
"Curiac vs. Abadie (1 d., 502.)

"Kierski vs. Mathews (1 d., 591).
"Thaver vs. Hedges (23 Ind., 141).
"Breitenbach vs. Turner (18 Wis., 140).
"Jones vs. Harker (37 Ga., 503).
"Renolds vs. Bank of the State (18 Ind., 467).
"Wilson vs. Trehiltock (23 Iowa, 331).
"Met Bank vs. Van Dyck (27 N. Y., 400).
"Hague vs. Powers (39 Barb., N, Y., 427).
"Roosevelt vs. Bull's Head Bank (45 Id. 571).
"Murray vs. Gale (52 Id., 427).
"George vs. Concord (45 N. H. 434).
"Van Husan vs. Kanouse (13 Mich., 303).
"Hintrager vs. Bates (18 Iowa, 174).
"Maynard vs. Newman (1 Nev., 271).
"Milliken vs. Sloat (Id., 573).
"Borie vs. Trott (5 Phil., Pa., 366).
"Johnson vs. Ivey (4 Coldw., Tenn., 608).

"History proves beyond a doubt that the emperor, king, parliament or congress can coin and issue money of any material and make such money a full legal tender within its own jurisdiction. If the high courts of nations have so declared and the Supreme Court of the United States, backed up by the state courts, has so affirmed, then the people of this Government should never allow

anything to circulate as money that is not a full
legal tender for all debts within its jurisdiction.
The issuing of money is a right too sacred to be
entrusted to the greed of corporate power. Therefore all money must be issued by the Federal
Government and all profits for its use go into the
treasury of the United States. The people have
delegated their sovereign powers to coin or issue
money to Congress. The Supreme Court has so
declared in its decisions. The issuing of one kind
of money made redeemable in another is a delu-
sion and a snare. If the money issued is a full
legal tender, then such money is the fulfillment
of the law, and, being the fulfillment of the law,
needs no redeemer.

"The people have placed the whole and
sovereign power in Congress, therefore Congress
may and must issue all money that the needs of
business require. It is the only source from
which money may come. It is issued by Congress
for the use of the people and by their authority
alone. Then let Congress fix a safe and sure security on which money is loaned—a security
which gold or silver, or both, are not, never have
been or never can be.

"Therefore be it enacted that the Secretary of the treasury shall issue directly to the people full legal tender money in such quantity as the business interests of the country demand and can use, at a fixed rate of interest not exceeding three per cent per annum, in perpetuity, at borrower's option on payment of interest, and secured by real estate, state, county and city bonds. This would prevent the possibility of panics and at the same time provide ample means for the support of the government without a taxgatherer in the land.

"Had Congress done its duty to the people that elected it and paid its salary, instead of bowing its head in humble submission to the bondholders and moneylenders of Europe and America, when this dark cloud of panic appeared, it could have dispelled it and prevented the bitter sufferings that the people have been and are still passing through. Congress could have ordered the Secretary of War to employ a sufficient number of civil engineers and have laid out good roads for twenty or thirty miles from every city in the country. This would have employed the idle labor. To build these roads Congress could have ordered the Secretary of the treasury to issue forty millions of full legal tender, each month. In six months this would amount to two hundred and forty millions or about three dollars and forty-three cents per capita. This amount paid to labor would have gone into the channels of business. The time lost by labor would have been sacred to the nation. The roads would have greatly benefited the people and increased the value of property in their vicinity. This would have stopped the panic and set the wheels of machinery in motion.

"Congress had the undoubted power to do this, but it did not. Hence millions of our people have suffered hunger and cold, and merchants have gone bankrupt. Shops, mines and factories have been idle, the knife of the suicide and the murderer have been sharpened, and the tidal wave of misery has swept over the nation. Before the bar of human justice Congress stands, accessory to the crime and misery brought upon the people by the panic, and could the hand of justice reach them they would not be in Congress, but in the penitentiary.

"But ever the right comes uppermost,
    And justice shall be done."

CHAPTER X.

"COLUMBIA'S ADVOCATE" was a special favorite of Mr. Trevellick. It is a pamphlet published in Washington, D. C. The September number of 1892, which he sent me, as a souvenir, contains in its "Theory of Laws" some of the ideas on financial and labor reform promulgated by him and his co-workers many years before the publication of the pamphlet. I copy a few of those reforms asked for and advocated by Mr. Trevellick.

1. That the government shall issue and supply directly to the people full legal tender money in such quantity as the business interests of the country demand and can use at a fixed rate of three per cent. per annum, in perpetuity at borrower's option, on payment of interest, and secured by state, county or city bonds or real estate liens.

2. Government ownership of railroads.

3.   A graduated income tax.

4.   Homesteads free from tax and exempt from execution.

5.   Telegraph and express rates reduced.

6.   Inside labor provided by the state for cripples and infirm.

7.   Spare time devoted to road making.

8.   Liquor selling prohibited by law.

9.   No banks of issue or National Banks.

10.   No government bonds in time of peace.

11.   All paper money to be government money.

12.   Eight hours a legal day's work.

13.   Navigable waters improved and canals made by general government.

14.   Arbitration in place of strikes.

15.   Co-operation among workmen where possible.

16.   Amalgamated trades unions.

17.   Free ballot for both sexes.

18.   Abolition of truck stores.

19.   Weekly payment of wages, in lawful money.

20.   No child labor under 14 years of age.

21. Free schools, free press, free religion, a pure judiciary.

22. No monopolies, no boycotts. Conciliation.

Such were some of the reforms advocated by Mr. Trevellick, and in the advocacy of them he grew exceedingly eloquent at times. He was no Utopian, and did not advocate impossible schemes. He well knew the many difficulties that reformers have got to contend against in this country, among which are the diversity of nationalities, of religion, of politics with all its jealousies and animosities engendered about the oft recurring election times. The diversity of language, all was injurious to the production of harmony among the workers. The great increase of the foreign born population and the spreading out and comparatively small increase of the native born or New England race, made it very hard to get the foreign born people properly assimilated. The large increase in the colored race and the great migration to the Northern states of people who only a few years ago, took no part in the management of the various governments in the cities, counties, states and nations, had a tendency to disintegrate and demoralize the efforts of the reform leaders who were trying to bring up the working people to a higher plane, by educating them in soberity, morality and good citizenship.

Trevellick spent his life and his money in studying standard authorities, and by comparing notes, analogy, and close observation he was enabled to arrive at pretty correct conclusions. The Bible says, "as a man thinketh, so is he," and Trevellick tried to direct men's thoughts aright. Again he tried to set a good example to his fellows. He wished to make them sharp and of quick perception to see why and how they were being deprived of a large share of the wealth which they were creating, that they and their families ought to have for their comfort and happiness. He sympathized greatly with those poor unfortunate men and women who had to get their living for themselves and those dependent upon their efforts. When he saw the hectic flush or the pallid cheeks of the poor women who had to pass most all her time in the illy ventilated factory, perhaps, bent down over her sewing machine or her nerves worked up to the highest tention by the whir and hum of machinery; and when he saw the poor miner going away down into the dark and dangerous bowels of the earth, in the morning, from which he would not return till after his children had gone to bed, oh how he longed to see the time of labor so shortened and services so well paid for, that those people should be able to breath the pure air, and bask in the beautiful sunshinhe, and see the bright flowers, and the limped waters of the brooks and rivulets, and hear the music of the feathered songsters in the woods and meadows. He knew that

> Man's humanity to man
> Made countless thousands mourn.

Feeling thus, he would feel interested in reading the following paragraph published in "Columbia's Advocate. It says:

"The history of the world proves that at all times, everywhere and under all conditions of mankind, in one way or another, a steady tendency to injustice towards the weak and inattentive has been shown by the strong, unscrupulous and vigilant, and that such encroachments have continued till unbearable and then followed by revolution, only to assume a new form and traverse a similar course to a similar end. The rise of nations is in efforts to establish justice, their fall comes from the denial of justice. How long it will be till the load of taxes and interest on the debts of the United States and of the people becomes unbearable, God only knows; but it cannot be long—and then, what?''

In 1860 there were no tramps; in 1892 there were legions. In 1860 there were not to exceed twenty millionaires; in 1892 there were over 30-000 persons who hold from one million to two hundred millions each. This is injustice, but it has been done under the operation of law governing the finances and commerce of the nation, which makes not cash but interest-bearing credit a basis of business, and gives to certain classes special privileges and monopolistic powers.

Let the genius of our laws be shown in contriving methods to provide means by which labor shall be employed, and not through neglect, lack of sympathy or of facility that it be oppressed.

The following from Ella Wheeler Wilcox, in Arena, seems very appropriate at this time:

The time has come when men with hearts and
    brains

Must rise and take the misdirected reins
Of Government, too long left in the hands
Of aliens and of lackeys.   He who stands
And sees the mighty vehicle of State
Hauled through the mire to some ignoble fate,
And makes not such bold protests as he can,
                    Is no American.

The highest conception of human nature is "a man," incomparable in all the virtues and graces which combine to make up this sublime character.   How wonderful in all the qualities which ennoble human existence and elevate the intellect above all inferior surroundings! How noble in action, when all human forces look up for a leader fit to comprehend and competent to act in an emergency; when real ability is demanded and true courage is required to supply the needs of the hour. In these days and in these prolific times, when opportunities are without limit, and human progress is operative in all directions, we should rejoice to behold a broad-chested unexceptional representative of this description, whose character, competence, liberality and achievement would at once challenge the public appreciation and win the support of all good men in politics, in society, in church and in state.

Such a man Trevellick could and would have been if his efforts were rightly appreciated. But he lived before his time.

Of course the large subsidized papers could not see any good in a Labor Reformer, and many of them wrote disparagingly of him and his work. And the working people are often apt to forget to applaud and reward their leaders who are risking their lives and reputations for their benefit. Instances of it may be shown at the present writing.

I have quoted these passages from Columbia's Advocate to show the trend of Trevellick's thoughts and actions. He would look at the great numbers of so-called tramps, and soliliquize thus: "Great goodness! Only think of the boundless resources of this country yet to be developed, and all this great crowd of young men turned out into the country to beg their bread, or steal, or starve. The idea is revolting, and the greater number of the tramps are of native birth and can speak the English language. Most of them have been taught to read, write and cipher in our pub-

lic schools. Strong, healthy, robust men, now
reduced almost to the level of brutes. Dirty;
many of them covered with vermin. Congregat-
ing and herding in police stations in winter and
in railroad cars in summer. Independence gone,
manhood gone, hope vanished, poverty and crime
staring them in the face. The iron gates of the
penitentiary ready to close on them, driven out
of the cities by the policeman's club. They are
verily like the Ishmaelites — their hands are
against every man and every man's hand is
against them. Seeming only to be waiting the
opportunity to band together in some time of
great excitement to become more avengeful than
the brutal hyena. Twenty-five thousand thieves
and pickpockets and burglars in New York alone;
whose very frequent home is the jail or penitentiary. See the enormous hordes of paupers and
inebriates fed by the labor of those at work, for
out of their labor and its productions comes all
taxation. Penitentiaries filling up and being en-
larged; houses of ill-fame increasing in number
faster than the increase of population. It is a
sorry sight in this, the greatest republic of modern
or ancient times. Where will it land us at last?

Either into despotic monarchy or revolution and anarchy.''

Trevellick would often in his lectures draw comparisons to illustrate his meaning I would refer to two in particular on the money question. Sometime about 1890, while lecturing in our city he spoke of the condition of finance in Venice when she was at the zenith of her power, and had the control of the commerce of the world at that time. Her bank was a safe bank of deposit and her paper money issued on the credit of the nation remained above par for over 600 years. When a man had gold or silver that he had acquired by trading with other nations, he took it to the bank and was given credit for it on its books. When he wanted money to use for domestic purposes or for local commerce he drew paper notes secured by the government, and the gold and silver was used to carry on foreign trade and to pay foreign debts.

Another illustration was that of the market house in the Island of Guernsy, in the English channel, in order to show how munincipalities could make improvements and provide labor for the people in slack times. The people of that

island once wished the government to build a
market house but he had no funds for that purpose. He started the work and issued what we
called scrip, or due bills, signed with the official
signature. They passed current for the labor
and material and the house was built; the stalls
were built and rented, and the building soon
brought in a revenue to the Island. The rents
were used to pay off the due bills and on a certain day the Governor issued a proclamation that their would be a great meeting of the
citizens in the suburbs of the city of St. Peters.
The people assembled amd the Governor made a
speech to them. He told them the market house
was out of debt and henceforth would be a source
of revenue to the Island. A box was then
brought out containing the scrip or due bills and
burnt up in a huge bonfire amid great rejoicing
by the people. Thus it showed how cities might
be improved with very little outlay of cash
money.

But Trevellick's greatest wish was to see
the shortening of the working day, and to show
the good results of the system. The Rev. Robert
Collyer, in writing on the subject after his re-

turn from England, showed conclusively that the adopting of the half holiday on Saturdays had proved a blessing to the working people of London. Saturday afternoons cheap excursion trains were run out of the various depots, filled with workingmen and their families, school teachers and their scholars, and factory girls by the thousand. They would run out 75 or 100 miles in the country and have a good picnic, amid the beauties of nature, in the fresh, fragrant, vitalizing air, laden with the ozone from the fields of clover or new-mown hay. They would return at night all cleaned up, and next day the churches and Sunday schools would be well attended. But if they had not gone on the excursion they would propably have been, many of them, in the gin-shops, and have spent Sunday in listless apathy, to say the least.

There is no excuse now for the employers. They once said that they could not afford to stop the machinery at eight hours—it would not pay; but now that they have the electric light they can work three shifts of men in twenty-four hours if they want to. It would give the idle men a chance to get work, and the money paid to labor would be widely diffused among the community.

CHAPTER XI.

TREVELLICK expressed himself as opposed
to the strike and the boycott as a very im-
perfect way of settling disputes among working
people and their employers. Yet he took part in
one boycott long before the word "boycott" came
into general use. (The word "boycott" was derived from the name of an Irish landlord who had
a dispute with his tenants, in which the tenants
got the neighboring trades-people to refuse to
trade or do business with the landlord.)

Shortly after Trevellick took up his residence in Detroit, and while he was president of
the trades-union there, a committee of working
girls waited upon him at his residence and stated
that they were dissatisfied with the prices they
were getting for the piece work that they were
doing in one of the workshops in the city, and requested him to try and get their pay increased.
He promised to do what he could. He promptly

went to the store and priced the goods that the girls were working on, both before and after they were made up into garments. Then after deducting the prices that the girls got for making, he found that the employer was getting too much profit over the labor performed by the workers, while they could not get enough to pay their board.

He therefore made a demand on the old man that he increase the pay of the women in his employ. He demurred and protested against any outsider or any union attempting to interfere in his business and flatly refused to make any change. So the next day boycott notices were published by the union. The result was that in a few days Dick was sent for by the old man, and he told him his business had fallen off a good deal and asked him to withdraw the boycott. Dick told him he must increase the scale of wages and sign a contract with the women's committee to that effect, and the old Hebrew did so.

On the following Saturday evening at the meeting of the trades-union Dick made his report and called on volunteers to go with him and buy something at that store. It was a gents' furnishing store and was also a factory. Almost every man went along, and for hours the clerks were exceedingly busy selecting and packing the purchases.

On Monday Dick received a note asking him to come to the store. He went and the old man took him into the office and set before him wine and cigars and was very much pleased that his trade had increased to such proportions through Dick's influence. Dick refused the wine but took a cigar.

The working women soon after presented him with a splendid gold ring with a suitable inscription engraved on the inside of it. He prized that ring very much and often wore it.

A few poems from a book which the writer received as a present from Mr. Trevellick some years ago, may be appropriate here, to illustrate his love for the thoughts expressed in them.

To the True Reformer:

List to thy thought, as its gentle voice greets
    thee;
And, sternly unshrinking, obey its behests:

Heed not the clamor of custom that meets thee;
  Still doing thy duty, leave Heaven the rest.

Cherish thy thought; 'tis a sapling upernal,
  Transplanted from Heaven, to flourish below;
Food fit for the gods it will yield thee eternal,
  Neglected, its fruit will be sorrow and woe.

Live to thy thought; be the model, God given,
    Thy guide, as the soul's walls from day to
      day rise.
Patiently build; thou shalt see unto Heaven
    A temple of beauty in grandeur arise.

Trust in thy thought; 'tis an anchor will hold
      thee
    From drifting, when storms of adversity
      blow;
Compass and chart when night's black clouds
      enfold thee,
    While steering thy bark from the islands of
      woe.

Utter thy thought; see thou lock not the coffer,
  Thus meanly and miserly hiding it there;
Out with it boldly, not fearing the scoffer,
  As bright as the snn, and as free as the air.

Follow thy thought; it will lead to the moun-
    tain;
  Thy soul shall then bask where the flowers
    bloom ever,
Drink blessed draughts at felicity's fountain,
  Rejoicing with friends that no future shall
    sever.

—

The Time Has Come.

The time has come to stand erect,
In noble, manly self-respect;
To see the bright sun overhead,
To feel the ground beneath our tread;
Unled by priests, uncursed by creeds,
Our manhood proving by our deeds.

The time has come to break the yoke,
Whatever cost the needed stroke;
To set the toiling millions free,
Whatever price their liberty;
Better a few should die, than all
Be held in worse than deadly thrall.

The time has come for men to find
Their statute book within the mind;

To read its laws, and cease to pore
The musty tomes of ages o'er;
Truth's golden rays its page illume,
Her fires your legal scrolls consume.

The time has come to preach the soul;
No meagre shred, the manly whole.
Let Agitation come; who fears?
We need the flood; the filth of years
Has gathered round us.   Roll then on.
What cannot stand had best be gone.

—

Labor.

'Tis the two-edged sword of sharpness,
      'Tis the boots of seven-leagued stride,
'Tis the stone that burns our pewter
      Into gold, twice purified.
'Tis the hymn all nature's singing,
      'Tis the prayer God loves to hear.
He who labors finds an answer
      To his supplications near.

—

What Makes a Man?

Not numerous years, nor lengthened life;
Not pretty children and a wife;

Not pins and chains and fancy rings,
Nor any such-like trumpery things;
Not pipe, cigar, nor bottled wine,
Nor liberty with kings to dine;
Not coat, nor boots, nor yet a hat,
A dandy vest, a trim cravat;
Not houses, lands, nor golden ore,
Nor all the world's wealth laid in store;
Not mister, reverend, sir nor squire,
With titles that the memory tire;
Not ancestry, traced back to Will,
Who went from Normandy to kill;
Not Latin, Greek nor Hebrew lore,
Nor thousand volumes rambled o'er;
Not judge's robe, nor mayor's mace,
Nor crowns that deck the royal race—
All these united never can
Avail to make a single man.

A truthful soul, a loving mind,
Full of affection for its kind;
A helper of the human race,
A soul of beauty and of grace;
A spirit firm, erect and free,
That never basely bends the knee;

That will not bear a feather's weight
Of slavery's chain to save a state;
That truly speaks from God within,
And never makes a league with sin;
That snaps the fetters despots make,
And loves the truth for its own sake;
That trembles at no tyrant's nod—
A soul that fears not even God;
And thus can smile at curse and ban—
That is the soul that makes a man.

—

Do Right.

'Tis wisest and best at all times to do right,
In brightness of sunshine, or darkness of night;
For sorrow and woe are companions of sin;
When virtue walks out they fly readily in;
No rest is there henceforth, by day or by night,
For him who has wandered away from the right.

Do right, in each heart says a sweet angel voice;
Obey, and in sorrow you still may rejoice;
A rill in your wanderings will always be nigh,
And there you may drink when the fountains are
          dry;
For joy, like an angel, is ever in sight,
To bless with her presence the doer of right.

Do right, tho' a crowd of mean cowards do wrong;
A child in the right is as Hercules strong.
The pathway is steep, and few travelers are there;
The prospect how pleasant, how balmy the air!
Then up, like the eagle that soars in its flight;
Heaven's mansions are built on the mountain of
    Right.

—

Be Thyself.

Be thyself; a nobler gospel
    Never preached the Nazarene.
Be thyself; tis Hóly Scripture,
    Tho' no Bible-lids between.

Dare to shape the thought in language
    That is lying in thy brain;
Dare to launch it, banners flying,
    On the boom of the main.

What though pirate knaves surround thee?
    Nail thy colors to the mast.
Flinch not, flee not, boldly sailing,
    Thou shalt gain the port at last.

Be no parrot, idly prating,
    Thoughts the spirit never knew;

Be a prophet of the God-sent,
   Telling all thy message true.

Then the coward world will scorn thee;
   Friends may fail and fiends may frown;
Heaven itself grow dark above thee,
   Gods in anger thence look down.

Heed not; there's a world more potent
   Carried in thy manly heart.
Be thyself, and do thy duty;
   It will always take thy part.

If the God within says, "Well done;"
   What are other gods to thee?
Hell's his frown; but where his smile is
   There is heaven for the free.

CHAPTER XII.

IN an interview held with Mr. Trevellick at Lincoln, Nebraska, January 10, 1894, a World-Herald representative quotes him as saying:

"In the year 1866 the heads of the various labor organizations met in Louisville, Ky. There were represented in that body the Shipcarpenters and Caulkers' Union of North America, the Printers' National Union, Stone Cutters' National Union, Bricklayers' National Union and Moulders' National Union. After five or six days' discussion on the misfortunes of strikes and the loss entailed to employer and employed, it was resolved to call a convention of all trades to meet the next year at Ford's theater, Baltimore. The convention met in June, 1867. After discussing matters in which they were interested, they appointed a committee of five to draw up a platform and resolutions on which it was supposed labor could unite, and calling the attention of the farmers of the nation to join us at our next gathering. The committee was appointed and the convention adjourned to meet in Chicago, in June, 1863. The platform read substantially as follows:

"'First. We demand that all money. whether metallic or paper, shall be issued by the Federal government and when so issued shall be a legal tender for all debts public or private.'

'"Second. We demand the abolition of National Banks as soon as their charters shall expire and no further renewal.'

"'Third. That all lands held by the Federal government should be held for actual settlers only; and all lands held by corporations up to that time and not entered by said corporation, their charters should be forfeited by reason of non-compliance with the law, and returned to the custody of the United States, and held for actual settlers only, that no land should be sold or granted to any person or persons not citizens of the United States or those who had declared their intention to become so.'

"'Fourth. We demand for women equal pay for equal work.'

" 'Fifth. That all children born under the United States flag, or brought to the United States, shall be compelled to receive a common school education.'

" 'Sixth. That we recommend that strikes never be entered into until all other means of settlement have failed.'

"These resolutions were drawn up in Detroit and presented to the committee in the town of Ionia, Michigan, in 1868, and we readopted. On presentation of the said resolutions, I presented copies to the following named gentlemen, and asked their approval or disapproval of the same:

"Judge David Davis of the Supreme Court of the United States, General B. F. Butler of Massachusetts, Wendell Phillips of Massachusetts, Peter Cooper of New York, Pliny Freeman of New York, Judge Sanford P. Church of New York, Governor Parker of New Jersey, Judge Thompson of Virginia, General Thomas Ewing of Ohio, Governor Booth of California, Hon. Alexander Campbell of Illinois, and Hon. John McGuire of Missouri.

"The replies of these gentlemen were read and all expressed satisfaction with the platform or

resolutions.   The resolutions were presented at
Chicago by Major Thomas Armstrong, of Pitts-
burg, late editor of the Labor Tribune, and were
adopted.

"A party was organized on that platform,
which party continued four years.   The president of the labor congress was empowered to ap-
point an officer in each state to assist him in organizing on that platform.   The persons appointed were T. V. Powderly of Pennsylvania,
George E. McNeil of Massachusetts, John Sin-
clair of New Hampshire. John Ennis of New
York, Wm. Burkley of Indiana, Andrew Cameron
of Illinois, George Claflin of Missouri, John
Sensenek of Michigan, Robert Gillchrist of Kentucky, and George Fetterman of New Jersey.

"One of the first persons elected to any office
under this new party was Senator G. N. Smith of
the present senate of Nebraska, being elected as
one of the selectmen of his own town in New
Hampshire.

"In the state of Pennsylvania the labor congress, or the Labor party, carried several counties, including Luzerne.   During the long fight
of two years in organizing the party in Pennsyl-

vania every officer, as soon as found to be an officer or member, was immediately discharged from his employment.   Three times Mr. T. V. Powderly was discharged and driven from one part of the state to another, but was afterward elected mayor of his own city, the city of Scranton, and re-elected for three full terms.

"At the end of four years the labor congress closed its work.   A new party was formed on the same platform called the Industrial Brotherhood. The Industrial Brotherhood existed for two years, and then gave way to the Greenback Labor reform party; still adopting the original platform.   The Greenback party, with the reform party, continued to use the platform for several years.   The first national nomination made on that platform was for president of the United States, Judge David Davis of Illinois; the second, Peter Cooper of New York; third, General James B. Weaver of Iowa; fourth, Mr. Streeter of Illinois.   During the last two years of the Greenback party Michigan elected a governor, and thirteen congressmen were elected at different periods.

"At this time a central committee was

formed in Illinois, of which the present congressman from Nebraska, Mr. McKeigan was chairman, and he, with several workers in the Greenback party, assisted in the nomination and final
election of Mr. Stevenson, vice president elect,
as congressman from the Bloomington district.

"During the years of the Greenback and
other parties under the same platform, the anti-
monopoly party was formed, and took its first
large start in Central Illinois; second a strong
organization was formed in the city of Omaha, in
which the late Judge Clinton Briggs of that city
took an active part. Out of these various names
came the People's party, and from the time of its
inception until the meeting of the Ocala conference no change had been made in said platform.
At that time, a large portion of the delegation
being from the Southern States, an addition to
the platform, known as the treasury plank was
presented.

"Thus from 1866 to 1892 the same platform
adopted and first given to the world on December
16, 1868, has remained, and is still, with the exception of the treasury plank, the same platform
that was not only adopted at the first convention,

but sanctioned by the gentlemen whose names are given above.

"It is pleasant on returning to Nebraska to find that in the present house and senate may be found two—one in each body—of the gentlemen who played a prominent part in the formation of the Labor Congress twenty-five years ago, namely, Senator Smith and Mr. P. H. Barry of the house; and it would be proper to state that no man wielded more effective service in the early working of the party than a citizen who is now well known in the state of Nebraska—John M. Devine of Colfax county, who was at that time secretary of the organization in Massachusetts.

"It is strange, but nevertheless true, that few men who avowed themselves believers in that doctrine have ever changed their faith, and it is also true that while party names have passed away the principles have gone forward until to-day there are organizations teaching that doctrine in every state and territory in the union, and at present the fate of five or six United States senators, or, at least, their election, depends on the vote of the people belonging to the new party.

"Many of the new converts are zealous in

the work, but have not studied the principles
which underlie their platform as carefully as
they should have done.   If I can find any fault
in Nebraska it is not that Nebraska has not true
men and lovers of the principles contained in their
platform, but I find here, as in many other states,
too many men who understand too little of the
platform ready to accept nominations, when they
have not carefully studied the principles of the
party to which they belong, and are, therefore,
unable to defend them as they should be defended.

"Notwithstanding the difficulties the founders
of this platform have had to contend with by
reason of lack of means, yet its growth is as-
tounding, and now that years have passed away
the question is often asked and hundreds of letters are received by me why it was, that at such
an early period after the war I should have written that platform.   My answer is as follows:

"No republic ever stood or ever can stand
after the farmers of that nation become tenants
at will of any man who may own the land.   I was
convinced then, as I am now that revolution is
ahead of us, and that in the near future.   Not a
revolution of force—God grant that may never

come—but a revolution is coming, and it is for the American people to say that it shall come by action of legislation and just laws.

"In 1862 when I left my home in the city of New York, 75 per cent of the inhabitants of those two great cities, Brooklyn and New York, owned a home.   I have lived to reach my 63rd year when only 18 per cent own a home in either of those two cities; and fully 70 per cent of the inhabitants of our great cities can say truthfully today, as the Master Christ said in the days of his flesh. 'The birds of the air have nests and the foxes holes, but the son of man has not where to lay his head.'   Every man born in America or he who emigrates to America and acquires a home, is a foundation on which the pillars of state firmly rest. But when by mortgage or accident that foundation is removed, a pillar of the state's safety has been broken; and at no time in the history of civilization has the loss of homes and farms been so rapid as in these United States in last twenty years. The state of Illinois, the brightest star in the galaxy of the agricultural flag, has already more tenant farmers than Scotland; and the United States has more tenant farmers than any other nation on the face of the earth.

"Another fact which cannot fail to strike the thoughtful observer is that the labor of America in field, factory and farm is paying interest to foreigners on at least 8,000,000,000. This is one of the reasons why such men as Terrence V. Powderly, Thomas Armstrong, Andrew Cameron and the Hon. William McKeigan of your own state have given so many hours of precious time in building up that which they believe would save the nation's life and bless humanity.

"Although political supremacy was not attained yet those efforts were not fruitless. The legal tenders issued to save the nation's life, which proved so potential and which demonstrated that the energies which God has placed in human muscle and brain, and the natural resources with which our land is blessed, need not be dormant, and the hope of liberty depart from the earth, unless vitalized by those substances of which only barbarians could make money. The money of civilization was saved from destruction. The pernicious clauses of the specie resumption act of 1875 were repealed. It was also made im-

possible that another charlatan should be crowned;
or that another Sherman be landed as a financier,
for putting millions into the pockets of his New
York syndicate, by selling notes signed by
60,000,000 of people, said notes bearing 4 and
4½ per cent interest, and forfeiting the right to
redeem them for thirty and forty years, by de-
monstrating that the bonds of the United States
could be placed at 3 per cent, with the right to
pay them by the government at any time.

"Following these results political agitation
calmed down and apparantly ceased altogether.
But the institutions inherited from the past
must necessarily force our people through all the
stages and ultimately compass their ruin and our
fate becomes like unto that of all former civilization, decline, decay, extinction. But other forces
are making themselves felt, for while the cun-
ningly devised scheme of the usurer was moving
on apparently successful in its mission to sap the
industrial life of the country and to gather in to
itself the ripe product of industry and enterprise,
a feeling of unrest and protest had been growing
throughout the land. This culminates in the full
developement of the Knights of Labor as an or-

ganization. There can be no question that the
principles taught by the Knights disseminated in
every corner of the land by its members, many of
whom, through removal or otherwise, while not
keeping up their active membership taught its
gospel in sections where its organization was
practically unknown, and prepared the way to
the wonderful awakening of the tillers of the
soil.

"First the oppressed laborers of every trade
are organizing and confederating, newspapers are
springing up in their defense. Time goes on.
At last the rainbow. of promise appears; a light
appears in every schoolhouse on the prarie, the
farmer by his occupation, isolated from his fellows, walking silently behind his plow during
the long weary day, hastens at eventide when
chores are all done to seek that rest his weary
limbs require, but now he hies him to yonder
schoolhouse, where he meets his neighbors to enquire the causes and find a remedy for the conditions which he sees so gradually but surely en-
compassing him, that the promise of the future
is anything but assuring. The alliance is a fact,
and from ocean to ocean and from lake to gulf,

the flickering light of lamp and candle from schoolhouse window light up the path of reform.

"What great force has put all those molecules in motion, spontaneous, simultaneous? It cannot be by accident. It is not a single neighborhood; it is the people.

"What do we behold next? The separated, isolated have moved and come together in the district school. We now behold them converging from all points of the compass. Ocala, Florida, is their objective point. Here were gathered men from every state in the Union. Here met the blue and the grey, but not to fight over the battles of the past. They met as friends, not enemies. One common purpose has drawn them together; the dark cloud of mortgage, gradually gathering and threatening to burst in ruin over their heads, had driven them to meet and seek in union and consultation the means of common safety. After days of consultation and discussion—through it ran the hope, and on the part of many, the belief that a formal withdrawal from the old parties would not be forced upon them, but that the reform indicated would be adopted by them—the convention reaffirmed the old plat-

form, with the addition of the so-called Ocala
sub-treasury plan. A year's waiting proved the
futility of this hope, and St. Louis again affirmed
the platform adopted at Ocala. In succession
came Indianapolis, Cincinnati, St. Louis again,
and finally Omaha, and here, having waited in
vain for years, the absolute necessity of the formation of a third party was shown, and a full
ticket was nominated and so, fully rigged and
manned, the ship was launched upon the stormy
seas of politics.

"And now a word as to our present condition. The solid south—kept so by the deceptive
actions of the Republican party, knowing as they
did that if the south could be kept solidly Democratic the perpetuation of the Republican power
was made certain—is no longer solid. The People's party has made it impossible, and at the
same time divided the great northwest, upon
which they had so fondly based their hopes for
continued power, and now that the People's party
holds the balance of power in the election of
United States senator in eight states. It is all-
important in the building up of the People's party
that Independents or Democrats should be elected

and thereby prevent the possibility of the Democratic party shielding itself behind a Republican
majority in the United States senate, and thus
enable them to again go before the public and
say: 'We did not bring the relief to the overbur-
dened producers which we promised in our last
campaign because the Republicans held a majority in the senate.'

CHAPTER XIII.

THE following is from the Chicago Tribune of June 30, 1888, headed "Dick Trevellick's Latest Reform:"

"DETROIT, MICH., June 24th.—Richard F. Trevellick, of this city, the grand lecturer of the Knights of Labor, and a specially candid, intelligent, and observant man, has returned from a trip to the far west, where he has been engaged among his fellow workingmen for several months. In speaking of some of the more important facts attracting his attention upon this trip he remarked:

" 'There is one great wrong in the western and northwestern states and territories that must sooner or later be righted by the general government, and the sooner the better, for it effects in some degree the welfare of all. The federal government, in reserving the right to control all navigable streams within its own jurisdiction, acted wisely in the interest of the whole people. In the west and northwest we find hundreds of thousands of acres of the richest of land depending upon irrigation for their production. These great interior basins of valuable land are surrounded by high mountain peaks, the tops of many of them perpetually crowned with snow. The snow clad mountains produce hundreds of beautiful streams which flow down to the valleys below, and must be used for irrigation by the farmers and gardeners or these vast valleys must become almost a barren waste. In almost every case these streams are controlled by corporations and their waters sold to farmers and gardeners at such an enormous price that the farmer and gardener must remain poor, no matter how productive the soil or hard they may work. Justice to the American people, and more especially to the farmer and gardener demands that these streams be purchased and controlled by the federal government in the interest of the whole people, and in no better way can a portion of the surplus money in the treasury be expended. In this way alone can the farmers and gardeners in these rich valleys become independent citizens of the government instead of the dependent subjects they now are and must ever remain if left dependent on the greed and caprice of these water corporations. This is especially true of parts of California, Colorado and Montana.

" 'In visiting the valleys of Montana I found some of the most picturesque and fertile valleys to be found in the world. The valley of the Gallatin is about fifteen miles wide and forty miles long. At the head of this valley the Missouri takes its rise, formed by the coming together of the three beautiful mountain streams—the Gallatin, Jefferson and Madison. The production of this valley is enormous, and could be greatly increased if the government would purchase the mountain streams and sell their waters to the farmers and gardeners at cost.

" 'It produces wheat, oats, potatoes and all vegetables and grasses in abundance. The foot-hills around it furnish excellent grass known as bunch or Buffalo grass, which feeds tens of thousands of cattle and sheep. Berries grow in great abundance when properly cared for and watered, notably the gooseberry, strawberry, currant and raspberry. Three tons of timothy hay are often produced to the acre.   The wheat grown in this valley will average over thirty bushels to the acre, often weighing from 64 to 66 pounds to the bushel, and in some cases wheat has been produced at from 65 to 70 bushels per acre.   Oats will average from 60 to 65 bushels per acre and in some cases have reached the enormous amount of from 105 to 110 bushels an acre, 44 pounds to the bushel.   Potatoes will average from 300 to 350 bushels an acre, and in some cases have reached 700 bushels.   It is not uncommon to see potatoes weighing from 4 to 4½ pounds.   White parsnips, carrots and mangel-wurzels will reach from 700 to 1,100 bushels an acre.   Onions grow in abundance and almost as large as Bermudas.

" 'There are several of these valleys in Montana and almost all of them are as productive as the Gallatin.   The largest and most productive are the Gallatin, the Deer Lodge, the Judith, the Prickly Pear and the Bitter Root.   In portions of Bitter Root and the Judith some varieties of apples are grown with great success.   These rich valleys are surrounded by the various mining camps of the mountains, producing copper, silver, gold and lead; coal is found in abundance.

" 'The principal mining camps are found in and around Butte City. Very large stamp, crushing and smelting works are found at Wickes, Anaconda, Butte and Blue Bird. Blue Bird mill is the largest dry stamp mill in the world, and is owned by Mr. John Lubbock, of London. These large works and mines give constant employment to over 50,000 men and furnish a ready market for all the production of the great interior valleys; and while this is true of Montana, it is equally true of the other states and territories of the great northwest, and readily shows the absolute necessity of the government purchasing the mountain streams in the interest of the whole people and thereby guarding the interests of the toiling masses against the rapacity of corporations.

" 'In these mountain regions and valleys there are 400 or 500 assemblies of Knights of Labor, composed of farmers, miners, mechanics and laborers. These in common with the Knights of Labor throughout the United States, and their allies, the Farmers' Alliance, the Farmers' Wheel and other labor organizations, desire that the government effect this reform, and do it speedily.' "

DEATH NOTICES.

The following notice of the Death of Mr. Trevellick was sent to the writer of this narrative by his son, dated February 20, 1895:

"Dear Sir:—When I returned last Thursday I found the blow had fallen. (Mr. Trevellick died from the second stroke of paralysis.) His end was as quiet and peaceful as his life had been stormy and troubled. It seems as if a kindly providence took him thus suddenly and quickly that he might not know that his life work was and must remain incomplete. But in another sense his work was rounded and complete. He did what he considered was his duty to do, and could do no more. The highest eulogies the Romans in their prime passed upon their departed men was, 'He has done his duty.'"

The following is from the Cleveland Citizen:

"Dick Trevellick is dead. A few years back he was one of the best known advocates of organized labor in the country. He came to the States from Australia in 1861 and took up his residence in Detroit, and, until recent years when he became an invalid, no man has worked more faithfully and earnestly for the cause of labor than Richard F. Trevellick. He will be remembered with gratitude by the army of labor exponents who push the work forward, as a pioneer who fought his way through the wilderness of prejudice and made a path for others to follow, and none will say the world is not better for his having dwelt among its people.''

The following is from the Joliet News of March 1, 1895.

"At the last meeting of the Populist Club the following resolutions of respect to the memory of R. F. Trevellick were adopted:

"WHEREAS, It has pleased the Divine Ruler of the universe to call from our midst one of the most patriotic defenders of liberty and the rights of man, one of the advocates of the religious rights of the citizens of the United States, and as great an investigator of the systems of human government as ever lived in the United States of America; Therefore,

"*Resolved:*   That in the death of R. F. Trevellick, the employers of labor have lost a friend, for he always respected the rights of invested capital and always claimed that the ballot box was the proper place to right all the wrongs of the working classes.

"*Resolved:*   That the laboring masses should always revere the memory of Trevellick, for the reason that he spent the best part of his days in advocating their cause and the sacred brotherhood of man.

"*Resolved:*   That we, the Joliet friends and admirers of the deceased brother, take this method of expressing our sincere sympathy with the members of the family of our old friend Trevellick, and of our regret for the loss of such a friend to the cause of reform in all kinds and conditions of the human race.

"*Resolved:*   That a copy of these resolutions be sent to the daily papers and also to the bereaved family of our deceased brother."

The following is from Editor G. Lynn, of

Our Own Opinion, Hastings, Nebraska, Feb. 20th, 1895.

"Dear Friend:—Yours of the 17th received. We saw a notice of the departure of our dear mutual old friend in the Omaha Bee. I wrote the dear, good, afflicted one, and sent for his little book. He sent me two. He was delighted to hear from me, and told me how little he had written for the last eight months. He was feeling chagrined and despondent at the manner our government officials were embarassing and bartering away the interests of the working men and women of the country. His letter was written on the 14th of the present month, and was the second last that he wrote, you having received the last one.

"He was a brave noble soul. There was no man in the country that stand so prominently in the foreground, for the organization of the industrial forces as R. F. Trevellick; in fact he was the foremost-writing out, formulating and defending the first platform of principles, in which the labor forces began to play an important part.

"That first declaration of sentiments showed the clear brain, and presence of mind of their author; advocating the indentical opinions in the main, that the advance guard of reform take today.

"We recollect what a power he was in our old greenback days—and fight. In his later years he lacked none of the earnestness, but much of his suavity. He grew impatient at the apathy and ignorance of the masses, and he felt like castigating them for their apparent readiness, (or indifference,) to wearing the chains the treasonable servants (whom they had elected to serve them) were helping the 'money power' to fasten on their minds and bodies.

"His heart was always right. No truer soul ever existed, no truer brain was exercised to free the people from the results of their own ignorance, moral cowardice, jealousy of each other, and base subserviency to the behests and demands of the Plutocracy. He has done his work, and done it well. It remains for us who are still in the body, to continue the battle in which he fought so valiantly."

The Detroit Gazette of March 29, 1895, published the following report of a meeting held in that city the Sunday previous. It read as follows:

"THE TREVELLICK MEMORIAL.

"In the absence of President O'Neil the meeting held at Trades Council hall last Sunday afternoon in honor of the memory of the late Captain Richard Trevellick was presided over by Thomas M. Dolan, the veteran cigar-maker. Mr. Dolan was a life-long friend of Captain Trevellick, and on being called to the chair paid a high tribute to his character and worth. The sincerity of purpose, the devotion to duty and the active work of Captain Trevellick were commended. Through his persistent efforts the national eight-hour law was adopted.

":John McVicar was the first speaker on the programme. He reviewed the history of labor organizations from the fourth century down to the present time, and closed with the following touching eulogy of the dead leader:

" 'It will be readily seen that the ardent youth of to-day, who, at 20 or 21, on initiation into his trades' union, expects the millenium for workingmen is at hand, is an optimist of optimists. Yet, while his pessimistic brother may think the millenium has not even a glimpse of dawn, there is much to encourage both. Trades unions have been productive of great good to the working people, not only to those organized, but, by their influence, to those unorganized.   Good in the matter of many kinds of protection, as well as in increase, or prevention of decrease, in wages. In an educational way their influence has been even greater.   In begetting in men a spirit of proper independence and self-assertion they have done a grand work.

" 'My personal knowledge of these facts has covered a period of one-third of a century, and during some thirty years of that time I personally knew the man whose memory we are gathered here to honor, and also know that no single individual did better work in aiding the results of trades unionism reached in Detroit than did Richard F. Trevellick.   Not only in Detroit was his influence felt, but throughout the United States.   He grandly fulfilled the injunction of the poet to the laborer:

'Stand up erect; thou hast the form
And likeness of thy God.   Who more?'

" 'And he possessed—

'A soul as dauntless, 'mid the storm

Of daily life, a heart as warm
And pure as breast e'er wore.'

" 'In fact, he was 'as true a man as moves the human race among.'

" 'I was a member of the old trades assembly in Detroit with Mr. Trevellick a quarter of a century ago.   Driven from his trade because of his unionism, he found a place to which he was well fitted.   Possessed of a strong physique, a grand voice, of quick perception, of ready speech, of beautiful imagery, he need only to study situations to clear conclusions from his great wealth of common sense, and with his powers of oratory lay them before his fellows, to set the latter to thinking and to action.   In the language of the same poet before quoted, it might be well said of him in life:

'True wealth thou hast not—'tis but dust,
    Nor place—uncertain as the wind;
But that thou hast, which with thy crust
And water, may despise the lust
    Of both—a noble mind.'

" 'Moving amongst us daily, Mr. Trevellick was well known, and was greatly beloved by those who knew him best.   He was a man of noble impulses, never a self-seeker, generous in assistance to others, a staunch friend, valiant and persistent for the right as God gave him to judge the right, earnest for the best interests of the people as he understood them; a man of positive convictions and pointed assertion, yet a man of peace, who believed in the wisdom of counciling together as opposed to anything partaking to violence, in all endeavors to reach adjustments of differences between capital and labor; a man ever willing to give corporations or employed capital all aid consistent with the proper protection of producers.

" 'With all these good qualities, however, Mr. Trevellick was not fully appreciated in life as he should have been, and I regret to say that this lack of appreciation was not confined to the classes or individuals from which it is least expected or wholly unlooked for, as applied to such men as our dear departed friend. The lack of appreciation was found in the ranks of labor, as it too often is in such cases.

" 'But I do not intend to go into that farther. Our friend is gone. Any regrets that he had not been given the meed due him in life are of no ser-

vice to him now.   But if there are any within
sound of my voice who feel such regrets, I know
they cannot please the spirit of Trevellick more
than to be less sparing of the proper appreciation
of others who similarly serve them in life, if the
spirits of departed friends can or do take cogniz-
ance of the acts of those they have left behind.

" 'Mr. Trevellick's virtues are well worthy
of emulation, and I sincerely hope the good seeds
sown so freely by him in their example, and also
in his speeches, may live and be productive of
good results that will redound to the benefit of
all in whom implanted, and through them to others
who never had the pleasure of his acquaintance or
the satisfaction of listening to his silver tongue
for an hour without realizing that fifteen minutes
had passed.'

"A letter from Mayor Pingree was read, in
which a peculiarly high tribute to the deceased
was paid.

"Speeches were also delivered by Alderman
Samuel Goldwater, Captain J. M. McGregor,
Robt. Y. Ogg, Wm. F. Abrams, C. O. Bryce, L.
E. Lossy and Judge Donovan.

"Wm. F. Abrams suggested that the meet-

ing should take the initiatory step towards raising
a fund to erect a suitable monument to the memory of Captain Trevellick, and the idea met with
unanimous approval.

"The following rosolutions were unanimously adopted by a rising vote:

" 'WHEREAS: Death has claimed one of the
most prominent members of the labor movement,
Captain R. F. Trevellick, who in the pioneer
days of labor movement defended the rights of
labor, both by voice and pen; and

" 'WHEREAS: By the death of Mr. Trevellick organized labor has lost a noble champion and
an earnest worker; therefore be it

" 'Resolved: That we who have known him
well and long, and, recognizing the sterling qualities of the deceased, mourn his death.

" 'Resolved: That we extend to the family of
the deceased our heartfelt sympathy in their be-
reavement.

" 'Resolved: That a copy of these resolutions
be sent to the family of the deceased by the secretary, with the assurance that the memory of

their departed friend will always remain green in the memory of those here assembled.'

"The following poem was prepared for the occasion by John Drew:

'Farewell to Trevellick, the friend of the toiler,
    The man who had always the workman in mind,
Who devoted a lifetime of work and of labor
    To breaking the fetters monopolists bind.

In days that were darkest in years now gone by,
    When labor lay prostrate and blacklists were
        rife,
He arose like a star of the morning to guide
    Through the darkness which hovered o'er or-
        ganized life.

Like the square and the compass, he ever was true
    To the cause wherein his heart was first set;
And the masses, when striving their right to assert,
    Will then think on his loss with regret.

Now his harvest has come, and he sleeps in re-
        pose—
Free from life's cares and turmoils and crashes.
And to-day, as we're gathered in memory's fold,
    We'll unite in saying 'Peace to his ashes.''

"The following was also dedicated to his

memory by M. Dando, of Braidwood, Ill.:

'The sturdiest oak in the forest has gone;
  The toilers' best friend has surrendered at last.
The talents no plutocrat ever could buy
  Have answered the summons of death's chilly
      blast.

That patriot, whose voice he ever raised in de-
      fense
Of workingmen's rights, and of labor oppressed,
Has eventually been silenced by the 'grim mon-
      ster' death,
  Amid the sympathy of toilers universally ex-
      pressed.

The name of Trevellick shall live through the ages
  As the foremost among heroes who battled for
      right,
As one of the wisest of counsellors and sages
  Who ever for justice was ready to fight.

His tongue that eloquently plead labor's cause
  Is silenced forever and shrouded in gloom;
The brain that conceived the thoughts that he
      spoke
  Now only inhabits the windowless tomb.

'Midst turmoil and strife, thy battle of life
  Is ended; thy troubles and sorrows will cease.
Death brings in its hand what was denied thee
        in life—
  Perfect rest and absolute peace.'

EULOGIES.

LA SALLE, ILL., Feb. 10th 1896.

Dear Sir:—If there is anything that would give me more pleasure than another, it is to testify to the honor, honesty and integrity of our old time friend Dick Trevellick. Dick, as we loved to call him, was a true genius. The first time I met him was during the troublous times of 1887. I had called a mass meeting of the miners of this district on the public square of this city. Being their president I wished to advise them on some matters of importance.

Just as we were going to commence, who should put in their appearance but old Dan McLaughlin and Dick. They were a happy sight. Dick was known to the entire mining fraternity, either personally or by reputation. They had no truer, firmer friend than he and he was compelled to get up at once and make them a speech. Dick was more than a speaker—he was a born orator. A thorough logician, a philosopher, a man of deep research, a student of human nature and society and of the material world of which he was a part. No man labored harder or more earnestly for human welfare than he did. His scanty recompense would have disgusted even an itinerant Methodist preacher.

While not a preacher of Jesus and Him crucified, yet he was one of His most exemplary followers. Jesus' motto of preaching in all the world and travelling without purse or scrip was well exemplified in old Dick. There was no thought of making a charge—he took whatever he got and was well content. He would go around with the hat and gather what he could, but no matter what it was Dick was satisfied. Had he turned his attention in other directions he would have been at the head of the social world. But there are always some brave souls who are willing to sacrifice both health and wealth for human well being. When in LaSalle he always stopped at my house. My wife thought Dick Trevellick the second Jesus Christ; there was nothing too good for him. He was sociable and kindly, full of every tender feeling and as passionately fond of children as he was of human

justice. He had a fund of knowledge on all subjects; could enter into the minutest details of
cooking; talk laws of geology, astronomy or any
other science. Had my wife been alive (she is
dead four years now) she would have reminded
me of many of his anecdotes. The last time he
was in LaSalle he stayed with us five days; that
time we had discussed nearly every known subject. As I said before he was passionately fond
of flowers and on Sunday morning he and I along
with some others (there were always visitors
when Dick was here) went down to Peter's
flower garden, through the hot house and exam-
ined the plants. Dick led the way and with his
cane pointed out the various flowers, told us the
family of plants to which they belonged, told us
what part of the earth's surface they were inde-
genous; gave us a real, practical lecture on bot-
any. It was a sight to see old Peter, the
gardener; his eyes bulged out with wonder to
think that a man should know so much of his
trade and yet not follow it. It was a great mys-
tery to him. That was one of the most pleasant
Sunday mornings I ever spent. A something
never to be forgotten; a sermon that few men

were privileged to hear, but which left a strong impression on every one present.   Time and again have I been reminded of it by some one and wondering when he would come back.   Dick was a true labor leader and of the school of Terrence V. Powderly.   My recollection is that he was in a great measure, if not entirely, the author of the preamble and platform of the Knights of Labor, of which he was a member.   Dick Trevellick and Terrence V. Powderly are my beau ideals of labor leaders.   Men whose personal example are worth a thousand sermons or ten thousand lectures.   Too many of our American labor leaders are given up to the whiskey habit—make a great speech and then go off and get drunk, but their preaching brings no good results.   Working men expect that their advocates, like their preachers, will keep sober.   A good speech without example is like a pair of shoes without soles.   There is after all nothing to walk upon but bare feet.

JOHN McLAUCHLIN.

Mr. McLauchlin was 15 years supervisor of the town of LaSalle and a member of the 39th General Assembly of Illinois.

CHICAGO, Feb. 28th, 1896.

I knew Capt. Dick Trevellick, as he was called, for twenty years or over, as the pioneer in the present great reform movement. He was a natural born reformer, a true patriot and lover of his fellow-men. As a public speaker of great eloquence and power, he was known to nearly every labor organization in the United States; and as an organizer and leader he had few equals. He was a faithful friend and a brave, unselfish champion of the cause of the people.

SEYMOUR F. NORTON,
Editor Chicago Sentinel.

MARSHALL, Texas, March 12, 1896.
O. HICKS,

Dear Brother:—I would gladly help you in the matter of which you write, but I did not know Capt. Trevellick personally. I am quite sure I never met him or if I did it was in such a casual way that I do not recall it and I do not think I could have forgotten meeting a man of his gifts and prominence. That I admired and honored him I need not say. He was a noble leader in the labor movement and will ever have the

gratitude and affection of all those who are helping to hasten the day when the hand of toil shall
hold the Helm of State.

Believe me, Yours in the Faith,

FRANCES E. WILLARD.

MILWAUKEE, WIS.

O. HICKS,

Dear Sir:—I had the pleasure of many years
of intimacy with Richard F. Trevellick, but as I
am not an adept at descriptive writing, I will
contribute a story or two toward your book.

When Moses W. Field was nominated for
Congress in Detroit in 1874 by the Republicans,
all the aristocratic members of that party left
him in the lurch because he had advocated the
cause of labor and currency reform and introduced an eight-hour bill in Congress.   I lived in
Cleveland, Ohio, at that time, and Field asked me
to come and speak for him.   When I arrived in
Detroit I found that all his own party speakers
had refused to help him, and he and Trevellick
were the only oratorical talent available.   The
first night Dick and I were billed to speak in the
same hall.   He had never heard me speak before,

but after I got through he came to me and taking my hand said:

"Bob, 'tis an infernal shame to waste two such speakers as you and I at one meeting, and as we have a large number of meetings arranged, we will divide up after this."

And we did. For two weeks Field, Trevellick and I made things boil in Detroit; and although not a Republican paper or a Republican speaker supported the candidate, Field came very near being elected. The joke on me was that I had just passed through a red hot campaign in Ohio, which voted in October in those days, and had been speaking for the Democrats and then went to Michigan to speak for the Republicans, and there was nothing inconsistent in that.

In Ohio, Bill Allen had been the Democratic candidate for Governor, and had declared that specie payments were a G—— d—— "barren ideality," and although I was a Republican I supported and voted for him because he represented progressive ideas. Field, who ran as a Republican, held the same views, but as soon as the reform party was organized he supported it.

Two years after, Brother Trevellick went to

Cleveland to deliver an address.   I was to intro-
duce him to the audience, and as we were ascending the pagoda in the public square, surrounded
by fully 2,000 people, Dick turned to me and said:

"Bob, tell me, for God's sake; what shall I
talk about?"

"Why," I replied, "you are to talk on labor
and currency reform."

"But I have spoken here so often that I cannot think of anything new on these questions that
I might say."

"Do you want my advice?" I asked.

"Certainly."

"Well, then, begin with the A, B C."

"Why, what do you mean?"

"I mean," was my answer, "that when you
start to speak, assume that there is not a single
solitary soul in the crowd that ever heard you before.   Start with the A, B C.   You are not talking to us who understand the question, but you
are talking to the unregenerated political hea-
then.   They know nothing about the issue; we
do.   Don't talk to us; talk to them."

"All right," said' Dick, "I'll take your advice." And then he launched out in that inimitable way of his. Argument, facts, description, jokes, pathos, alternating so rapidly that the audience was laughing until the tears ran down their cheeks one minute, and the next tears of sympathy would take the place of laughter. For over three hours he kept that crowd standing in the open air, and made one of the most effective speeches of his life.

In his death the reform movement sustained a serious loss. He had a voice that was simply magnificent, and when he presided over the National Convention of the Reform Party in 1880 he demonstrated that he was one of the few, the very few, in the country whose voice was adequate to the occasion.

His life and death were typical of the fate of all reformers in the world. Men are like a cow that will not enter a new stable, except by dint of great labor and effort. Men will not adopt anything out of the old ruts, and those who point out new ways and improved methods will be treated as cranks and fools by their fellows. Men have always crucified their saviours and honored them after death. Richard F. Trevel-

lick was one of the crucified ones. Born with
wonderful natural talent, not alone as an orator
but as an organizer, grim poverty not only prevented him from developing the latent genius in
his youth, but prevented its expansion after he
reached mature years.

Those who should have been his best friends,
who should have held up his hands, were the
greatest drawbacks to his welfare, and he died in
comparative poverty, after having labored all his
life, not for self, but for humanity.

ROBERT SCHILLING.
Editor Milwaukee Advance.

BRAIDWOOD, ILL., Feb. 6., 1896.
Dear Sir:—It gives me great pleasure to
know that you have undertaken to write up the
life and eminent services of our deceased friend,
R. F. Trevellick. It would be much satisfaction
to me if I could contribute anything that would
aid you in this noble work, and if I could give
expression to emotions created within me upon
every occasion when listening to the words of
eloquence and wisdom as they fell from the lips
of that great labor leader and agitator, I could

fill quite a space in your volume, but words fail
me and I will leave it to abler pens than mine.
I believe it was in 1871 or 1872 that I first saw
and heard Mr. Trevellick speak in this city at a
meeting of miners called for the purpose of
strengthening our Union. The lumber for the
erection of the Grove school building had been
brought to the prairie and the pile of lumber for
this first school building in District No. 2 was
converted into a platform where the speaker stood
and spoke for nearly two hours, holding the vast
audience in rapt attention. Even at that early
time he seemed to see with prophetic vision the
great and manifold wrongs that the laboring and
producing masses would have to endure in these
later days. He spoke of the vast influence
wielded by the money power, its control over
legislation and by bribery and corruption, se-
curing the passage of laws that were only beneficial to themselves and detrimental and oppres-
sive to producing people of our nation; he spoke
of the baleful and blighting sway of the money
power in causing the people's representatives to
place the exceptions on the second issue of Green-
backs, the people's money, and thereby depre-

ciating our medium of exchange; of Congress, in
behalf of the Gold-Clique, making custom dues
and interest in our National debt payable in gold
and thereby giving to that clique an opportunity
to fleece the people by selling their yellow money
at their own price. The speaker also dwelt at
some length upon the high crimes and misde-
meanors of our public servants in connection with
the Pacific railroads and the "Credit Mobiler"
and the slimy trail of the "Serpent," right up to
the Executive mansion. Of the millions of acres
of land given away to corporations whose members were distinctly proven to be the people's
representatives in Congress. The speaker was
at that time as I ever knew him afterwards, a
thorough Greenbacker, a believer in Government
paper money, and of said money being made a full
legal tender for all debts, both public and private;
he strongly urged upon his hearers the absolute
necessity of thorough organization in order to be
better prepared by united effort to resist the
attacks that he prophesied would be made by the
money powers upon the rights and liberties of
the common people. His speech upon this occasion created a profound impression upon the

audience and upon no one more than the writer
and for some time thereafter the subjects of his
speech and the speaker was the principal topic
of conversation among the miners of this locality.
The seed sown on that occasion bore good fruit
for a while, but some fell upon stony ground
and when the old politicians, servants of party
and of the money power came around with honied
words, great promises and their effective weapon,
money, the miners and producers were divided
and the parasites who live upon the earnings of
others which control both old parties, won the
battle and the oppression of the producers by the
interest consuming class, so eloquently described
by the speaker Trevellick, had received further
confirmation.

I am not positive of the date of the next visit
of Mr. Trevellick but I know he came here in the
fall of 1877 shortly after the ending of our great
strike in that year; he spoke in Braidwood on
Saturday evening and on Sunday was at my
house, and on the following Monday evening I
drove over to the Diamond mines in his company,
where he spoke to a mass meeting of miners in
McGurk's hall.   His speeches made upon this

occasion, as upon every other visit to our city, (which were either four or five) were of the most eloquent and pathetic nature, and always demanded the closest attention of his audience throughout. He was a master of oratory and had his talents been devoted to the interests of the capitalist class, instead of the down trodden laborers he would have ammassed a fortune and have been considered a successful man by those who measure success by the number of dollars possessed. But like all honest reformers, he had a severe struggle with poverty and an uphill fight against the cunning of the money power and their political harpies, the two old twin parties. And even where he should have received unanimous support, political, financial and moral; among the toiling massses in whose cause the very best years of his life were spent, he received only indifferent recognition. But my pen fails me to even in part, describe the eloquence, pathos, and burning zeal with which this devoted man applied himself to the work of upholding the interests of the toiler and to emancipate him from the thraldom and greed of his oppressors. I am glad therefore that the task of perpetuating his name and transcribing the life work of this noble man, has been taken up by one of his old comrades who will, I am sure, do justice to the work he has voluntarily assumed. I am sure there was no greater, better, truer or Nobler man than our departed friend R. F. Trevellick.

MESHO DANDO,
Police Magistrate.

INDIANAPOLIS, July 3, 1896.

MR. O. HICKS, Joliet, Ill.

My Dear Sir:—I am exceedingly pleased to learn that some good friend, knowing the high character, wonderful attainments and noble impulses of our deceased friend, Richard F. Trevellick, is about to write his biography. I am sure it will be indeed gratifying to the men who have been in the labor movement since 1850 and who often had the pleasure of meeting this manly man, this eloquent exponent of labor's rights, Richard Trevellick. The work he performed in his time in the interest of labor laid the basis for the superstructure of our labor movement of to-day. Too much credit cannot be given him. And I am pleased to lay this small expression of my sentiment upon his tomb as a simple tribute in honor of his memory.

Very Truly Yours,

SAMUEL GOMPERS.

President American Federation of Labor.

TERRE HAUTE, IND., April 4, 1896.

Dear Sir:—Your favor of the 3rd in reference to the life of Richard F. Trevellick has been received. While I never had the pleasure of meeting Mr. Trevellick in person, I knew him well by the splendid services he rendered to the cause of labor. He was a pioneer in the reform movement and as such achieved prominence by years of courageous championship of the rights and interests of the oppressed and down-trodden. I am glad to know that a record is to be made of his life work. I am sure it will not only be an interesting addition to the labor literature of the times, but that it can be read with profit by every student of the industrial conflict of the past and present. Mr. Trevellick worked hard and faithfully to better the condition of workingmen, and like all of his kind builded better than he knew. His work will survive him and he will be remembered with gratitude by thousands and thousands yet to come. I am only too happy to add my humble tribute to his memory.

Yours Very Truly,
EUGENE V. DEBS.

SPRINGFIELD, ILL., April 2, 1896.

Dear Sir:—Responding to yours of the 20th ult. would say that I was never sufficiently familiar with the life and efforts of Richard F. Trevellick to warrant me in going into details respecting his work in behalf of the eight-hour movement. While I knew him personally, we met but seldom. So far as I knew, his life was one continued strife in the interest of the wageworkers of this country. I hope that your efforts in presenting his life work to the American people will be crowned with success. When the book is published please send me a copy with bill.

GEORGE A. SCHILLING.

Secretary Bureau of Labor Statistics.

JOLIET, ILL., March 28, 1896.

Dear Sir:—You have requested me to write a few remarks in commemoration of the late Capt. Trevellick.

To Capt. R. F. Trevellick, more than any other man in this country, the laboring masses are indebted for the reduction of the hours of labor from twelve to ten hours. Years ago when working at his trade in England and America he made strong speeches in favor of shorter hours of labor, and then claimed that 8 hours for work, 8 hours for sleep and 8 hours for rest or recreation was what nature intended for man.

I got acquainted with Trevellick about 20 years ago at a labor meeting held in this city. And I shall never forget the surprise he gave all who heard him. Capitalists were surprised because he respected the rights of invested capital and its full protection under the law. Workingmen were surprised because he denounced strikes which he said rarely settled grievances and when it came to a question between a rich corporation and a lot of poor workingmen as to which had the deepest flour barrel, it could be easily seen who would win.

He surprised me because I, in common with all others, expected to hear a blood-thirsty address and an appeal to the passions and not to the brains and intelligence of his hearers. Ah! there

was where poor Dick excelled;   he would not and
could not be purchased to influence the masses
other than what he believed was for their best
interests.

I often heard you speak of his matchless oratory and magnetism over masses of men, and I
had an excellent chance to hear him at the labor
convention in Chicago in 1880, which nominated
Weaver for president.   About a thousand red-
hot delegates from all parts of the United States
attended that convention.   The question was,
who is capable of wielding the gaval over that
body of men?   Trevellick was chosen and a grand
choice he was, for he charmed them by his eloquence and his manly presence, and the magnetism of the man over that assembly was simply
superb, showing that he was a born leader of
men.   To show the magnetism of the man over
an audience, I wish to relate an incident in connection with that convention.   The second day of
the convention he was requested to consult with
the committee on platform, and he put Judge
Stubbs of Iowa, a fine appearing old gentleman, in
the chair.   In a short time pandemonium was let
loose.   The convention became very soon into an

uproar, and it was laughable to see the state of
affairs when the Captain returned. Trevellick
on that day proved himself truly a captain of men.
He at once ordered the seargeant-at-arms (Denis
Carneg of California) to clear the aisles, and every
man to take his seat. He inquired of Judge
Stubbs the proper order of business and soon
everything was serene.

The last time he was here he delivered a sermon in the Universalist church on the duty of
workingmen in particular to observe and respect
the sacredness of the Sabbath, which so charmed
and electrified his hearers and so pleased the
pastor that he invited Dick to come every time he
was in Joliet.

Trevellick is gone, and it will be a long time
before the working classes will have a leader like
him, for many reasons which space forbids me to
state. I am an Irishman born, he an Englishman
born, yet I loved him as a brother, which shows
that liberty makes brothers of us all.

He lies on the romantic banks of the St. Clair
river at Detroit, in sight of the flag of his native
country and under the glorious stars and stripes.
From his resting place can be seen the ships

which he loved so well, carrying the commerce of his country to and from the great west.

The angels of peace and justice, which were his talismen, will well sentinel the tomb, and the wierd winds from heaven will sing requiems to his memory till crack of doom.   And nature will lovingly spread its verdant mantle over the old hero. And the diamond dew drops which bedeck his grave in the gray of the morning are only symbolical of the tears and everlasting love of a grateful people.   To me how apt the lines:

"Seven cities claimed great Homer dead.
Through these seven cities Homer begged his bread."

JOHN RYAN.

Ex-Chief Fire Department.

RACINE, WIS., JULY 18, 1896.

MR. O. HICKS,

Dear Sir:—I can truthfully say that it affords me the greatest pleasure to comply with your request for a testimonial of the appreciation of the life work of Mr. R. F. Trevellick.   I first met Mr. Trevellick at Utica, N. Y., in 1867.   He was then on his way to attend the annual meeting of the National Labor Union at Philadelphia, of which he at that time was the vice president. I was at that time in my 23rd year and was presiding officer of Lodge 17, Knights of St. Crispin, which numbered upwards of 350 members.

He stopped off and spent Sunday with me, and left with the understanding that I should solicit the aid of the active workers of the other labor organizations to get up a public meeting, that he might address the workingmen of that city on his return journey from Philadelphia. I succeeded in complying with his request to the extent that a large audience was gathered to meet him at the appointed hour. He was the first speaker that I had ever heard on the labor question outside of my own lodge room. And it was listening to that which caused me to take up the cause of the wage workers and make it a study. I shall never forget it.

He was then in his 36th year and in the full vigor of his young manhood. It was the first lecture on that subject that had ever been given in that city, and was a surprise to the people. The idea that a mechanic should be able to stand up before a crowded hall full of people and enter-

tain them for more than two hours on economic
questions was considered marvelous, and it was
the talk of the city for days afterward.   It was
from his lips on that Sunday afternoon that I received my first lesson in what at that time was
called the labor movement of the United States.

At that time one could count on his fingers'
ends the number of workmen that could hold the
public platform for an hour and entertain an audience.   The case at the present time is different,
and there was no man who has lived in the last
half of this century who has contributed more to
bring about the change than Richard F. Trevellick, and had he devoted that talent to his own
selfish ends his children to-day might be in better
circumstances than they are.

He, I think, from his 35th to 55th year,
talked to more working people than any man on
the American continent.   If a dispatch came to
him to go across the continent to deliver a speech
on the labor question he responded as quick as if
it was only a few miles away.   And his heart was
the biggest part of his body.   He was never so
happy as when he was instructing and educating
the working people with a view of improving

their condition, and he was always willing to share his last nickle with them.   This debt to him can never be paid, and we can truthfully say that the world is better for his having lived in it.

Were I to subscribe a motto for Richard Trevellick I would do it thus: "I expect to pass through this world but once.   Any good, therefore, that I can do, any kindness that I can show to my fellow human being, let me do it now, let me not defer nor neglect it, for I shall not pass this way again."

RALPH BEAUMONT.

JOLIET, ILL., JULY 21, 1896.

I fully concur in the statements of Mr. Hicks as to the prominent position occupied by Mr. Trevellick among reformers.   Casting in my lot with labor reformers in 1851, I was always watching the men at the front.   Trevellick soon loomed high among them, and kept up.   It is true that platform compiled by him formed the basis of all our subsequent platforms.

But it was as a stump speaker that he made the greatest impression.   His imposing presence, tremendous voice, sound sense and clear logic made him the most effective all-round labor-green-back speaker we had during all the years he was in the field. He had that peculiar combination of faculties that enabled him to keep in the field and earn some sort of a living by making speeches through dry, hard, dull times, when every other reform speaker had to go into dry dock.

There was a dignity·and mastery of his sub-ject about Trevellick that made his utterances weighty, not only with wage workers, but also with the more thoughtful and patriotic of our mercantile and professional classes.

I met him a number of times and he was al-ways the same "glorious Dick"—unswerving, unpurchasable, indomitable, imperturable. Sound common sense invariably characterized his utter-ances. He was always in the-middle-of-the-road. There was nothing cranky about him, no fanati-cism, bigotry or craft. A plain, bluff, heart-of-oak English tar.

At the reform convention in 1875, whither I had come to head off Horace H. Day's foolish scheme to get himself nominated for President in 1876, Day's satellites kept me in the anteroom all the first day. When Trevellick, Bob Schilling and the other real leaders came they soon had me inside and Day was squelched.

At that tremendous convention in Chicago that finally nominated Weaver in 1880, I was very uneasy till Trevellick was made permanent chairman; then I knew that we would be safe. That was the sort of confidence that was felt in him by all the reformers. I think he never had any enemies among us, and no one was jealous of him.

His was "the voice of one crying in the wilderness: 'Prepare ye the way of the Lord; make his paths straight.'"

SAMUEL LEAVITT.

APPROPRIATE POEMS.

On polished springs true men of honor move;
Free is their service and unbought their love.
When honor calls and danger leads the way,
With joy they follow and with pride obey.
Not all the threats or favors of a crown,
A prince's whisper, or a tyrant's frown
Can awe the spirit or allure the mind
Of those who to strict honor are inclined.

—

To Trevellick.

O fairest pattern of a falling age,
Whose public virtue knew no party rage,
Whose private name all titles recommend—
The noble son, fond husband, faithful friend.
In manners plain, in sense alone refined;
Good without show, and, without weakness kind.
To reason's equal dictates ever true,
Calm to resolve and constant to pursue.

In life with every social grace adorned;
In death by friendship, virtue and honor mourned.

—

Farewell to Trevellick, my old carftsman, fare-
    well.
May we meet soon again, in the mansions above,
Where no battles or storms can ever expel
    The joys of the loved ones who meet there in
    love.

Hoist your light to the mast and sound well your
    gong
    To guide us safe into the haven of rest;
And send angels to meet us with music and song,
    On the evergreen shore, to live with the blest.

You have hewn to the line and your work proven
    true.
Your compass has guided you right to the point.
Your square and your plummet, as the work grew,
    Have shown that your genius was true as a
    joint.

Your anchor is down, your ship is secure—
    Now throw out your search-light, illumine the
    shore,

To show us the quicksands and rocks lying there,
  And warn us of dangers and bring us safe o'er.
Our old ship of state is in danger again;
  There are breakers ahead, mutineers at the
    helm,
They will scuttle the ship and will not refrain
  To pull down the colors and the crew over-
    whelm.

American freemen are things of the past;
  Injunctions and bayonets have cowed them at
    last.
The flag they fought under now trails in the dust;
  Bond shackles have bound them — surrender
    they must.

But a bright star of hope in the east is arising—
  The ship that you launched is now on the sea.
With her bells now a-ringing, joy she is bringing,
  At her mizzen-peak flying the flag of the free.
At the helm is Bryan, from the prairies arose;
  Tom Watson at the throttle, his hand on the
    wheel:
Seymour Norton on board, he stands now in re-
    pose,
  And Peffer throws the log and has charge of
    the reel.

The ship—she is staunch and she'll weather the
     storm;
  She is bowling along with the wind on the
     beam;
She'll weather the breakers—she's now in good
     form,
  And we'll bring her in harbor with her sails
     and her steam.

Then hurrah for Trevellick, that builder so true,
  Who fashioned the model and the patterns so
     good.
May she never surrender the red, white and blue,
  And triumphantly carry us over the flood.

                       O. HICKS.

American Labor: From Conspiracy to Collective Bargaining

AN ARNO PRESS/NEW YORK TIMES COLLECTION

SERIES I

Abbott, Edith.
Women in Industry. 1913.

Aveling, Edward B. and Eleanor M. Aveling.
Working Class Movement in America. 1891.

Beard, Mary.
The American Labor Movement. 1939.

Blankenhorn, Heber.
The Strike for Union. 1924.

Blum, Solomon.
Labor Economics. 1925.

Brandeis, Louis D. and Josephine Goldmark.
Women in Industry. 1907. New introduction by Leon Stein and
 Philip Taft.

Brooks, John Graham.
American Syndicalism. 1913.

Butler, Elizabeth Beardsley.
Women and the Trades. 1909.

Byington, Margaret Frances.
Homestead: The Household of A Mill Town. 1910.

Carroll, Mollie Ray.
Labor and Politics. 1923.

Coleman, McAlister.
Men and Coal. 1943.

Coleman, J. Walter.
The Molly Maguire Riots: Industrial Conflict in the Pennsylvania Coal Region. 1936.

Commons, John R.
Industrial Goodwill. 1919.

Commons, John R.
Industrial Government. 1921.

Dacus, Joseph A.
Annals of the Great Strikes. 1877.

Dealtry, William.
The Laborer: A Remedy for his Wrongs. 1869.

Douglas, Paul H., Curtis N. Hitchcock and Willard E. Atkins, editors.
The Worker in Modern Economic Society. 1923.

Eastman, Crystal.
Work Accidents and the Law. 1910.

Ely, Richard T.
The Labor Movement in America. 1890. New Introduction by Leon Stein and Philip Taft.

Feldman, Herman.
Problems in Labor Relations. 1937.

Fitch, John Andrew.
The Steel Worker. 1910.

Furniss, Edgar S. and Laurence Guild.
Labor Problems. 1925.

Gladden, Washington.
Working People and Their Employers. 1885.

Gompers, Samuel.
Labor and the Common Welfare. 1919.

Hardman, J. B. S., editor.
American Labor Dynamics. 1928.

Higgins, George G.
Voluntarism in Organized Labor, 1930-40. 1944.

Hiller, Ernest T.
The Strike. 1928.

Hollander, Jacob S. and George E. Barnett.
Studies in American Trade Unionism. 1906. New Introduction by
Leon Stein and Philip Taft.

Jelley, Symmes M.
The Voice of Labor. 1888.

Jones, Mary.
Autobiography of Mother Jones. 1925.

Kelley, Florence.
Some Ethical Gains Through Legislation. 1905.

LaFollette, Robert M., editor.
The Making of America: Labor. 1906.

Lane, Winthrop D.
Civil War in West Virginia. 1921.

Lauck, W. Jett and Edgar Sydenstricker.
Conditions of Labor in American Industries. 1917.

Leiserson, William M.
Adjusting Immigrant and Industry. 1924.

Lescohier, Don D.
Knights of St. Crispin. 1910.

Levinson, Edward.
I Break Strikes. The Technique of Pearl L. Bergoff. 1935.

Lloyd, Henry Demarest.
Men, The Workers. Compiled by Anne Whithington and
Caroline Stallbohen. 1909. New Introduction by Leon Stein
and Philip Taft.

Lorwin, Louis (Louis Levine).
The Women's Garment Workers. 1924.

Markham, Edwin, Ben B. Lindsay and George Creel.
Children in Bondage. 1914.

Marot, Helen.
American Labor Unions. 1914.

Mason, Alpheus T.
Organized Labor and the Law. 1925.

Newcomb, Simon.
A Plain Man's Talk on the Labor Question. 1886. New Introduction
by Leon Stein and Philip Taft.

Price, George Moses.
The Modern Factory: Safety, Sanitation and Welfare. 1914.

Randall, John Herman Jr.
Problem of Group Responsibility to Society. 1922.

Rubinow, I. M.
Social Insurance. 1913.

Saposs, David, editor.
Readings in Trade Unionism. 1926.

Slichter, Sumner H.
Union Policies and Industrial Management. 1941.

Socialist Publishing Society.
The Accused and the Accusers. 1887.

Stein, Leon and Philip Taft, editors.
The Pullman Strike. 1894-1913. New Introduction by the editors.

Stein, Leon and Philip Taft, editors.
Religion, Reform, and Revolution: Labor Panaceas in the Nineteenth
Century. 1969. New Introduction by the editors.

Stein, Leon and Philip Taft, editors.
Wages, Hours, and Strikes: Labor Panaceas in the Twentieth Century.
1969. New introduction by the editors.

Swinton, John.
A Momentous Question: The Respective Attitudes of Labor and Capital. 1895. New Introduction by Leon Stein and Philip Taft.

Tannenbaum, Frank.
The Labor Movement. 1921.

Tead, Ordway.
Instincts in Industry. 1918.

Vorse, Mary Heaton.
Labor's New Millions. 1938.

Witte, Edwin Emil.
The Government in Labor Disputes. 1932.

Wright, Carroll D.
The Working Girls of Boston. 1889.

Wyckoff, Veitrees J.
Wage Policies of Labor Organizations in a Period of Industrial Depression. 1926.

Yellen, Samuel.
American Labor Struggles. 1936.

SERIES II

Allen, Henry J.
The Party of the Third Part: The Story of the Kansas Industrial Relations Court. 1921. *Including* **The Kansas Court of Industrial Relations Law** (1920) by Samuel Gompers.

Baker, Ray Stannard.
The New Industrial Unrest. 1920.

Barnett, George E. & David A. McCabe.
Mediation, Investigation and Arbitration in Industrial Disputes. 1916.

Barns, William E., editor.
The Labor Problem. 1886.

Bing, Alexander M.
War-Time Strikes and Their Adjustment. 1921.

Brooks, Robert R. R.
When Labor Organizes. 1937.

Calkins, Clinch.
Spy Overhead: The Story of Industrial Espionage. 1937.

Cooke, Morris Llewellyn & Philip Murray.
Organized Labor and Production. 1940.

Creamer, Daniel & Charles W. Coulter.
Labor and the Shut-Down of the Amoskeag Textile Mills. 1939.

Glocker, Theodore W.
The Government of American Trade Unions. 1913.

Gompers, Samuel.
Labor and the Employer. 1920.

Grant, Luke.
The National Erectors' Association and the International Association of Bridge and Structural Ironworkers. 1915.

Haber, William.
Industrial Relations in the Building Industry. 1930.

Henry, Alice.
Women and the Labor Movement. 1923.

Herbst, Alma.
The Negro in the Slaughtering and Meat-Packing Industry in Chicago. 1932.

[Hicks, Obediah.]
Life of Richard F. Trevellick. 1896.

Hillquit, Morris, Samuel Gompers & Max J. Hayes.
The Double Edge of Labor's Sword: Discussion and Testimony on Socialism and Trade-Unionism Before the Commission on Industrial Relations. 1914. New Introduction by Leon Stein and Philip Taft.

Jensen, Vernon H.
Lumber and Labor. 1945.

Kampelman, Max M.
The Communist Party vs. the C.I.O. 1957.

Kingsbury, Susan M., editor.
Labor Laws and Their Enforcement. By Charles E. Persons, Mabel Parton, Mabelle Moses & Three "Fellows." 1911.

McCabe, David A.
The Standard Rate in American Trade Unions. 1912.

Mangold, George Benjamin.
Labor Argument in the American Protective Tariff Discussion. 1908.

Millis, Harry A., editor.
How Collective Bargaining Works. 1942.

Montgomery, Royal E.
Industrial Relations in the Chicago Building Trades. 1927.

Oneal, James.
The Workers in American History. 3rd edition, 1912.

Palmer, Gladys L.
Union Tactics and Economic Change: A Case Study of Three Philadelphia Textile Unions. 1932.

Penny, Virginia.
How Women Can Make Money: Married or Single, In all Branches of the Arts and Sciences, Professions, Trades, Agricultural and Mechanical Pursuits. 1870. New Introduction by Leon Stein and Philip Taft.

Penny, Virginia.
Think and Act: A Series of Articles Pertaining to Men and Women, Work and Wages. 1869.

Pickering, John.
The Working Man's Political Economy. 1847.

Ryan, John A.
A Living Wage. 1906.

Savage, Marion Dutton.
Industrial Unionism in America. 1922.

Simkhovitch, Mary Kingsbury.
The City Worker's World in America. 1917.

Spero, Sterling Denhard.
The Labor Movement in a Government Industry: A Study of Employee Organization in the Postal Service. 1927.

Stein, Leon and Philip Taft, editors.
Labor Politics: Collected Pamphlets. 2 vols. 1836-1932. New Introduction by the editors.

Stein, Leon and Philip Taft, editors.
The Management of Workers: Selected Arguments. 1917-1956. New Introduction by the editors.

Stein, Leon and Philip Taft, editors.
Massacre at Ludlow: Four Reports. 1914-1915. New Introduction by the editors.

Stein, Leon and Philip Taft, editors.
Workers Speak: Self-Portraits. 1902-1906. New Introduction by the editors.

Stolberg, Benjamin.
The Story of the CIO. 1938.

Taylor, Paul S.
The Sailors' Union of the Pacific. 1923.

U.S. Commission on Industrial Relations.
Efficiency Systems and Labor. 1916. New Introduction by Leon Stein and Philip Taft.

Walker, Charles Rumford.
American City: A Rank-and-File History. 1937.

Walling, William English.
American Labor and American Democracy. 1926.

Williams, Whiting.
What's on the Worker's Mind: By One Who Put on Overalls to Find Out. 1920.

Wolman, Leo.
The Boycott in American Trade Unions. 1916.

Ziskind, David.
One Thousand Strikes of Government Employees. 1940.